Windows on the World

ESSAYS ON AMERICAN SOCIAL FICTION

C. Hugh Holman

THE UNIVERSITY OF TENNESSEE PRESS
KNOXVILLE

Clothbound editions of University of Tennessee Press books are printed
on paper designed for an effective life of at least 300 years, and binding
materials are chosen for strength and durability.

Library of Congress Cataloging in Publication Data

Holman, Clarence Hugh, 1914–
    Windows on the world.

    1. American fiction—20th century—History and
criticism—Addresses, essays, lectures. I. Title.
PS379.H643   813'.03   78-13241
ISBN 0-87049-264-0

To Verna

Contents

Preface

Every novel is a window on the world, but the location, size, and even purpose of those windows differ immensely. As Henry James wisely said: "The house of fiction has in short not one window, but a million—a number of possible windows not to be reckoned, rather; every one of which has been pierced, or is still pierceable, in its vast front, by the need of the individual vision and by the pressure of the individual will. These apertures, of dissimilar shape and size, hang so, all together, over the human scene that we might have expected of them a greater sameness of report than we find. They are but windows at the best, mere holes in a dead wall, disconnected, perched aloft; they are not hinged doors opening straight upon life. But they have this mark of their own that at each of them stands a figure with a pair of eyes, or at least with a field-glass, which forms, again and again, for observation, a unique instrument, insuring to the person making use of it an impression distinct from every other. He and his neighbours are watching the same show, but one seeing more where the other sees less, one seeing black where the other sees white, one seeing big where the other sees small, one seeing coarse where the other sees fine." In this series of essays I concentrate most of my attention on windows that look out on a social world.

The novel is, I believe, an art form that finds its locus somewhere between an exclusive concern with an exterior, material world and a total immersion in a single, totally absorptive self. At one extreme we find Daniel Defoe's *Robinson Crusoe*, which, as Dickens noted, "exhibits a man who was thirty years on that desert island with no visible effect made on his character by that experience." At the other extreme, we find Dorothy Richardson's *Pilgrimage*, in which we never escape from Miriam's stream of consciousness into any material reality. Almost all fiction finds a place somewhere between these extremes, with the public world and the private self in some kind of balance, however unstable, and with the business of the novel consisting in significant part of the interaction of one upon the other.

The novel, in most of its forms—both important and trivial—has been a serious concern to me for most of my life, and for the past thirty years I have studied it with reference to three chief interests: the novel as it has been written in the southeastern United States, the historical novel, and the novel in which the social world has been a very important element. The three are not mutually exclusive, of course, but I have explored the first two in *Three Modes of Southern Fiction*, *The Roots of Southern Writing*, *The Loneliness at the Core*, and *The Immoderate Past*. In this volume I am bringing together eleven essays on the novel in relation to the social world.

Perhaps a word is in order about the sequence in which I present the essays in this volume. The first two deal with realism as a mode or genre of American fiction, and represent efforts to get at what Realism was as a movement in America between 1875 and the First World War. The next two essays deal with kinds of humor in the novel, with a special emphasis on satiric humor. The next two essays are on the work of John P. Marquand and Ellen Glasgow, novelists who wrote in the tradition of the novel of manners. They are followed by four pieces that deal with special aspects of the work of Glasgow, William Faulkner, and Thomas Wolfe. The concluding essay is an attempt to find a pattern in some American novels of development and to speculate on why it is there.

Most of these pieces originated as talks which I delivered on special occasions or as essays written under special circumstances. I am bringing together the present version of them because I think that they may say collectively some of the things which I have come to believe about the social novel in a quarter of a century of thinking about it.

"Literary Realism: An American Mode," "Faulkner's August

Avatars," "The Southern Provincial in Metropolis," and "The *Bildungsroman,* American Style" are published here for the first time. "Of Everything the Unexplained and Irresponsible Specimen" was published in the fall, 1964, issue of the *Georgia Review.* "Detached Laughter in the South" (© 1978 by the Board of Trustees of the University of Illinois) was published in *Comic Relief: Humor in Contemporary American Literature,* edited by Sarah Blacher Cohen and published by the University of Illinois Press. "Anodyne for the Village Virus" was published by Rutgers University Press in *The Comic Imagination in American Literature,* edited by Louis D. Rubin, Jr., in 1973. "Marquand, Novelist of Manners" was published as University of Minnesota Pamphlet on American Writers, No. 46, in 1965. "April in Queenborough" was published in the spring, 1974, issue of the *Sewanee Review* and also in *Ellen Glasgow: Centennial Essays,* edited by M. Thomas Inge and published by the University Press of Virginia, in 1976. *"Barren Ground* and the Shape of History" was published in Spring, 1978, issue of *The South Atlantic Quarterly.* "The Dwarf on Wolfe's Shoulder" was published in the Spring, 1977, issue of the *Southern Review.*

To the people who created the occasions out of which the original forms of these essays came, and to their publishers in previous appearances, who have granted me permission to reprint them, I am most grateful. When I realize that portions of six of them were originally given in symposia arranged by Louis D. Rubin, Jr., I am reminded once more of the good fortune I have enjoyed in being associated with this fine scholar and critic. I am grateful to Kenneth Cherry, former editor of the University of Tennessee Press, for persistence in asking me to assemble these papers, and to Mrs. Dinah S. Lloyd for her customary fine assistance in getting the pieces ready for the press.

Chapel Hill, N.C.   C. Hugh Holman

Acknowledgments

"Of Everything the Unexplained and Irresponsible Specimen':
Notes on How to Read Realism," by C. Hugh Holman,
was first published in the *Georgia Review*, 18 (Autumn 1964),
© 1964 by the University of Georgia, and is reprinted by permission of the *Georgia Review*.

"Marquand, Novelist of Manners," was first published as *John P.
Marquand*, University of Minnesota Press Pamphlets on Ameri-
can Writers No. 46, © 1965 by the University of Minnesota
Press, and reprinted by permission.

"Anodyne for the Village Virus" was first published in *The
Comic Imagination in American Literature*, edited by Louis D.
Rubin, Jr., © 1973 by Rutgers University Press, and used by
permission.

"April in Queenborough: Ellen Glasgow's Comedies of Manners" was first published in the *Sewanee Review* 82 (Spring
1974), © 1974 by the University of the South. Used by permission of the editor.

"The Dwarf on Wolfe's Shoulder" was first published in the
Southern Review 13 (April 1977), © 1977 by the Louisiana
State University. Used by permission.

"*Barren Ground* and the Shape of History" was first published
in the *South Atlantic Quarterly* 77 (Spring 1978), © 1978 by
Duke University Press. Used by permission.

Windows on the World

Windows on the World

It is one of the responsibilities of the novel to chronicle small desolations. These are sold short in that harsh artifice of selective recall we set down as history. Whose birthday party was cancelled by the fires that leaped over Troy? Who, on the Friday after Robespierre's execution, paid the laundress who had kept the great man's linens starched? What notes of felicitation, bitingly missed, what letters of condolence waited for by the hurt, impatient heart went to oblivion in the mailbags of the Titanic? In the troves and vestiges of Pompeii, it is the form of a dog wide-eyed with terror, still chained to his post, that numbs the spirit. The skein of experience woven of these threads, of the immemorial weight of the particular—the appointment never kept because of some sovereign irrelevance (what breakfasts stood uneaten, what gardens untended on St. Bartholomew's Day?), the toys on the palace floor, the frocks worn only once before becoming the legacy of the wind.

—GEORGE STEINER, "Unsentimental Education,"
New Yorker, August 15, 1977

Literary Realism: An American Mode

It is perhaps a sign of our fundamental sense of insecurity that the critics and historians of our national literature have of late sought persistently to find a single controlling principle that has governed literary expression in America. And since there is no area where the monition, "Seek and ye shall find," is more simply and readily applicable than it is to the criticism of literature, it is hardly surprising that such controlling principles have been found, or that, being found, they present violent contrasts to each other.

Charles Feidelson has seen American writing in the nineteenth century as an expression of the "symbolic imagination," a natural consequence of the American tradition which was, he thinks, the product of German idealism playing on Puritan methodology. Richard Chase defined "a native tradition" of the American novel, a tradition which he believes to be "its perpetual reassessment and reconstitution of romance within the novel form." He uses *romance* as a word, he says, which signifies "besides the more obvious qualities of the picturesque and the heroic, an assumed freedom from the ordinary novelistic requirements of verisimilitude, development, and continuity; a tendency toward melodrama and idyl; a more or less formal abstractness and, on the other hand, a tendency to plunge into the underside of consciousness; a willingness to abandon moral questions or to ignore the spectacle of man in society, or to consider these things only indirectly or abstractly."

Leslie A. Fiedler's *Love and Death in the American Novel* explicates the thesis that "the failure of the American fictionalist to deal with adult heterosexual love and his consequent obsession with death, incest, and innocent homosexuality are not

3

merely matters of historical interest or literary relevance. . . .
There is a pattern imposed both by the writers of our past and
the very conditions of life in the United States from which no
American novelist can escape, no matter what philosophy he
consciously adopts or what theme he thinks he pursues." On a
more cheerful note, R.W.B. Lewis has seen the central figure in
nineteenth-century American literature as the American Adam,
a primitive innocent in his New World Eden. R.P. Blackmur,
collecting a group of representative American novels, introduced them as all being in some form allegory, and said, "I
think that they [are] so because allegory is germane to their sensibility and appropriate to the culture they represent. Allegory
is how they set the things of the mind in motion so as to make
their words meaningful beyond themselves."

Joel Porte, in *The Romance in America*, has found the romance to be the predominant form for the nineteenth-century
American novels. Daniel G. Hoffman, in *Form and Fable in
American Fiction*, has seen the folk tradition as dominant.
David W. Noble has explored *The Eternal Adam and the New
World Garden* as "the central myth in the American novel since
1830." These examples are merely representative of general
treatments; if one moved to more limited or specialized studies,
the examples would greatly multiply, for there is a distressing
tendency to find the "key" to a single work and believe it to be
the "key" to many works. For example, William C. Spenge-
mann, in his 1977 study *The Adventurous Muse*, made some interesting discoveries about the importance of travel-writing in
America before 1900, then saw travel-writing pitted in a Mani-
chaean struggle against the evil domestic romance, and declared, "The competition between adventure and domesticity
for ideological and formal hegemony in American fiction is perhaps the most important single event in the history of American
literary nativism." The novel becomes for him "travel-writing
in its most literary guise," and he credits travel-writing with
playing a major role in "the evolution of symbolist aesthetics in
America," with being "primarily responsible for advancing the
authority and value of individual experience in literature," and

with being a significant influence on "the evolution of auto-biography." One is only mildly surprised to find that Spenge-mann's model romantic novel of adventure is James's *The Ambassadors*.

Spengemann is an exaggerated case of the tendency to fit the corpus of American fiction into a single frame. But all of these views share two attributes: they find submerged (and often unconscious) meanings beneath the surface of our major nineteenth-century writers, and they use these hidden mean-ings as a schema around which the rich complexities of art are ordered, reduced, and simplified. These critics often seem to be making a backward transfer by which they saddle the past with the neuroses of the present. Leon Howard once remarked, "To list all the symbolic and psychological interpretations of *Moby-Dick* would be to call the roll of most of the bugbears haunting the minds of modern intellectuals." In a sense, these critics are visiting the sins of the children upon the fathers even unto the third and fourth past generations.

This trend in contemporary criticism results in large mea-sure, I think, from two causes. In the first place the practice of literary history has fallen into some dispute, with the result that the awareness that it is necessary to look at the total picture has been lost. Every one of these critics has apparently felt justified in selecting a group of books which demonstrates his thesis and ignoring many others that do not. In the second place, the very healthy admonition to look at the work as in itself it truly is— the fundamental position which happily revolutionized the teaching of literature in post-World War II generations—has been followed blindly enough to allow the critic a freedom from the limiting facts of the world in which the work was pro-duced or the aesthetic theory out of which it came. Thus, hot for certainties in this our time, we brush aside impatiently the dusty answers that history gives and seek to make the past not a complex record of itself but a mirror for the present.

I believe that realism as it was self-consciously practiced by the American novelist in the last half of the nineteenth century was the literary mode that most adequately embodied the assumptions of the thoughtful American of *that* time, as existential romanticism seems to embody the assumptions of ours. The major tenets of realism were called forth by the postulates of the American dream; at its apex realism proved to be a reasonably accurate expression of that dream; and the decline of realism into doctrinaire naturalism, symbolism, and expressionism in our century has been the result in part of a decline in an active faith in that dream. This position is, I believe, in accord with the facts of literary history.

There are numerous and varied strands which make up the American experience, and there have been many traditions of life and art maintained by Americans at different times in our history. We are a people of deep complexity and rich variation, and we have produced art forms which reflect the complexity of our own nature. In respect for the scientific method, we have come, I fear, to assume that the truth resides in the simplest possible answer, in the broadest abstraction, in the grandest generalization, and in certain areas, notably the natural sciences, this is true. The very nature of the arts, however, demands that their truth be seen as a totality, a complexity, without reduction. When the rich stream of human experience is being presented, the greatest density and complexity rather than the greatest simplicity are essential to approximating the truth.

Walt Whitman Rostow in *The United States in the World Arena* sees as a powerful force in American history what he terms "our traditional national style." This style took its definitive shape in the years between 1815 and 1900, although its formative period reaches back to the early seventeenth century. As Rostow sees it, the American is basically an unphilosophical person, a creature of action and reaction; as a result the circumstances of geography, economics, and daily life have done more than systems of thought have done in making his distinctive style. Oliver Wendell Holmes once said, "The life of the law has not been logic; it has been experience"—an accurate description of the American style. This nineteenth-century American was, Rostow asserts, "an extreme empiricist and pragmatist, untheoretical and non-abstract in his thinking." Daniel

Boorstin has for some time been interpreting our history in this same way.

Such views of the American experience point to its relativistic and empirical nature. Yet the typical American, although he probably seldom thought of them, actually acted in the nineteenth century from a series of assumptions, so implicitly present in most of American life that our friends from abroad regularly saw them as definite characteristics. These qualities are the ones which find expression, I believe, in realism, a literary form in which the intrinsic oppositions of the American character found for a time an unstable but very real equilibrium. I think they are: the Puritan passion for righteousness; a pragmatic view of value; an egalitarian democratic sociopolitical ideal; a distrust of tradition, ritual, and ceremony; and a desire to achieve objectivity and to act with disinterest. The nineteenth-century American environment produced individualism, materialism, and hard-headed practicality, qualities essential to the nineteenth-century American character and to what William H. Whyte, Jr., calls "The Protestant Ethic," but it also produced a strong social and political moral sense, and it struggled in its art forms to express these qualities. The realistic novel was the form in which these qualities for a time found most nearly complete expression.

Realism is, in the broadest sense, simply fidelity to actuality as it is represented in literature; it is loosely synonymous with verisimilitude; and in this sense it has, of course, been a significant element in almost every school of writing in human history. In the more precise definition in which I am using it, however, it refers to the Realistic Movement which arose in the nineteenth century, at least partially in reaction against romanticism; which was centered largely in the novel; and which was dominant in France, England, and America from about the middle of the century to its closing decade, when it was replaced by naturalism. In this sense, realism defines a literary method, a philosophical and political attitude, and a particular kind of subject matter. Realism was called "nothing more and nothing less than the truthful treatment of material" by one of

7

its most vigorous American advocates, William Dean Howells, but the statement means little until the realist's concept of truth and his selection of materials are designated. Generally, the truth the realist seeks to find and express is relativistic, a truth associated with discernible consequences and verifiable by experience. Generally, too, the materials the realist elects to describe are the common, the average, the everyday. Furthermore, realism is a middle-class art, and it finds its subjects in bourgeois life and manners.

Where the romanticist transcends the immediate to find the ideal, and the naturalist plumbs the actual to find the scientific laws which control its action, the realist centers his attention on the immediate and here and now, the specific action, and the verifiable consequence. This distinction—the basic distinction among these three ninetenth-century literary modes—may be illustrated in this way. Imagine that we have a block of wood and a force of some measurable sort pushing upon it, producing in it a certain acceleration. The romanticist will tend to see in the entire operation an illustration or symbol or suggestion of a philosophical truth and will so represent the block, the force, and the acceleration—often with complete fidelity to fact—that the idea or the ideal that it bodies forth is the center of interest; in other words, he will treat the actual event not as important in itself but as a symbolic representation of a transcendent truth. The naturalist will tend to see in the event a clue or a key to the scientific law which undergirds it and to be interested in the relationships among the force, the block, and the produced acceleration, and will so represent the operation that Newton's second law of motion—even on occasion in its mathematical expression, as $F = ma$—will be demonstrated or proved by this representative instance of its universal occurrence in nature; in other words, he will treat the event not as important in itself but as representative data useful in the formulation of general statements regarding scientific behavior. The realist will tend to concentrate his attention on the accurate description of that particular block, that special force, and that definite acceleration, carefully eschewing tendencies to transcend or to generalize. The obligation he will feel was well expressed by George Eliot, in chapter 17 of *Adam Bede*, when she said, "my strongest effort . . . is to give a faithful account of men and things as they have mirrored themselves in my mind. . . . I feel as much bound to tell you as precisely as I can what that reflection is, as if I were in the witness box narrating my experience on oath."

Thus the realist espouses what is essentially a mimetic or imitative theory of art, centering his attention in the thing imitated and asking for something close to a one-to-one correspondence between the representation and the subject. He usually has, however, a powerful interest in the audience to whom his work is addressed, feeling it to be his obligation to deal with them with absolute truthfulness. Furthermore, the realist is unusually interested in the effect his work has on the audience and its life. Howells, concerned with his audience of young ladies, felt so strongly the obligation not to do them moral injury that he shut the doors of his own works to most of the aspects of life connected with passion and sex. George Eliot declared, "I would not, even if I had the choice, be the clever novelist who could create a world so much better than this, in which we get up in the morning to do our daily work, that you would be likely to turn a harder, colder eye on the dusty streets and the common fields—on the real breathing men and women, who can be chilled by your indifference or injured by your prejudice; who can be cheered and helped onward by your fellow-feeling, your forbearance, your out-spoken, brave justice."

The realist eschews the traditional patterns of the novel. In part the rise of realism came as a protest against the falsity and sentimentality which the realist thought he saw in romantic fiction. Life, he felt, lacked symmetry and plot; fiction which truthfully reflected life should, therefore, avoid symmetry and plot. Simple, clear, direct prose was the desirable vehicle and objectivity on the part of the novelist the proper attitude. The central issues of life viewed in this way tend to be ethical—that is, issues of conduct—and fiction should, therefore, concern itself with such issues, and—since selection is a necessary part of any art—select with a view to presenting these issues accurately

as they affect men and women in actual situations. Furthermore, the realist values the individual very highly and tends to
make characterization the center of his work. Hence, he has a
great concern for the effect of action upon character, and a tendency to explore the psychology of the actors in his stories. In
Henry James, perhaps the greatest of the realists, this tendency
to explore the inner selves of characters confronted with complex ethical choices earned him not only the title of "father of
the psychological novel" but also "historian of fine consciences."

The surface details, the common actions, and the minor
catastrophies of a middle-class society constituted the chief subject matter of the movement. Most of the realists avoided situations with tragic or cataclysmic implications. Their tone was
often comic, frequently satiric, seldom grim or somber, even
when situations have—as they often do in Henry James's novels
—tragic overtones.

That the old art forms, particularly the epic poem and the
romantic novel, would ultimately prove insufficient wineskins
for the new wine of burgeoning American democracy was a fact
recognized early in the nineteenth century. James Fenimore
Cooper, with a powerful sense of fact and a deep democratic
fervor, found the demands of the romantic historical novel to
be severe handicaps. In 1828, in *Notions of the Americans*, he
was willing to accept the idea that "the literature of England
and that of America must be fashioned after the same models
. . . so far as taste and forms alone are concerned," with the result that he found the American writer to suffer badly from
what he called "the poverty of materials." "There are," he declared, "no annals for the historian; no follies (beyond the most
vulgar and commonplace) for the satirist; no manners for the
dramatist; no obscure fictions for the writers of romance; no
gross and hardy offenses against decorum for the moralist; nor
any of the rich artificial auxiliaries of poetry. . . . I have never
seen a nation so much alike in my life, as the people of the
United States, and what is more, they are not only like each
other, but they are remarkably like that which common sense
tells them they ought to resemble." Thus the first major roman-

tic novelist in America found the materials and assumptions of American life unsuited to the romantic novel.

Nathaniel Hawthorne, in the Preface to *The Blithedale Romance*, in distinguishing between the Romance and the Novel, defined the novel in terms which are essentially those of realism. The novel "is presumed," he stated, "to aim at a very minute fidelity, not merely to the possible, but to the probable and ordinary course of man's experience." The greater freedom of the romance, Hawthorne felt to be the property of "the old countries . . . [in which] a certain conventional privilege seems to be awarded to the romancer." "Among ourselves," he lamented, "there is as yet no such Faery Land. . . . This atmosphere is what the American romancer needs. In its absence, the beings of imagination are compelled to show themselves in the same category as actually living mortals." And Herman Melville, caught by the nature of his theme and his subject, apologized in *Moby-Dick* for making the lowly the subject of romance. He declared, "If, then, to meanest mariners, and renegades and castaways, I shall hereafter ascribe high qualities, though dark; weave round them tragic graces; if even the most mournful, perchance the most abandoned, among them all, shall at times lift himself to the exalted mounts; if I shall touch that workman's arm with some ethereal light. . . . Bear me out in it, thou great democratic God!"

That this new world with its egalitarian view of man would find the old epic hero and the old extravagant action of traditional literature ultimately unsuited to its vision of experience, a perceptive French visitor, Alexis de Tocqueville, saw in 1831. In his *Democracy in America* he wrote: "Among a democratic people poetry will not be fed with legends or the memorials of old traditions. The poet will not attempt to people the universe with supernatural beings, in whom his readers and his own fancy have ceased to believe, nor will he coldly personify virtues and vices, which are better received under their own features. All these resources fail him; but Man remains, and the poet needs no more. The destinies of mankind, man himself taken aloof from his country and his age and standing in the presence of

Nature and of God, with his passions, his doubts, his rare propensities and inconceivable wretchedness, will become the chief, if not the sole, theme of poetry among these nations."

When Whitman invited the Muse to migrate from Ionia and desert "snowy Parnassus," he warned her that she would come "striding through the confusion," and would have to be

> By thud of machinery and shrill steam-whistle undismay'd,
> Bluff'd not a bit by drain-pipe, gasometers, artificial fertilizers,
> Smiling and pleas'd with palpable intent to stay,
> [She would be] installed amid the kitchen ware!

But the large example of Whitman's *Leaves of Grass* is to show that the Muse newly come to American shores will have not only to put up with the machinery of a growingly industrial society but will have to fashion its epics and its romances around "the single, separate person," whose most valuable characteristic is that what he assumes you shall assume and that for every atom belonging to him, as good belongs to you. If Aeneas is the embodiment of imperial Rome, and his poem the epic expression of Roman genius; then Whitman's generic "I" is the embodiment of democratic America and his poem the closest thing we have yet attained to an epic expression of the American genius.

The problem that Whitman wrestled with—that of formulating art from the average, the commonplace—was the problem that the novelist too wrestled with. And when the realistic novel finally enthroned the commonplace, representative middle-class protagonist at its heart instead of the romantic hero, an inevitable tendency in American life had reached its culmination.

Another nineteenth-century characteristic of the American was the absence in him of a sense of the past. In a sense the archetypal American protagonist is the perpetual stranger riding out of nowhere into a dusty western town, where no one asks about his past, where the problems of the moment engage him totally, and where at the end he rides away again, still a stranger and going no one asks where. The only significant dimension is extension in space, not in time. The American experience has been thus peculiarly centered in the immediate moment. Few of us look backward very far with impunity, outside the South where a concern with history has been persistent. The tasks before most Americans frequently appear as though they were in a vacuum, and we approach them with the sense of immediate and expedient obligation. This quality in our lives results in a degree of freedom from philosophical questioning. We have traditionally worried little about cosmology, and have been willing to say readily with Macaulay, "Metaphysics bakes no bread." Although in the nineteenth century we embraced the future with optimistic faith in the inevitability of progress, we have spent little of our time in the study of teleology. Our concern has been with ethics, with conduct. Our philosophical questions have tended to be epistemological—how do we know? Our answers from the beginning have tended toward pragmatism, toward a philosophy of values measured in terms of consequences. This pragmatic value system, together with a freedom from a sense of history, has given us an empirical view of life and has made us impatient with questions and concerns whose demonstrable results appear not to matter. When the realist centered his attention on the actual world as the center of value, asked that it be seen steadily and whole, and that it be presented with absolute accuracy and without reference to either transcendent ideas or underlying laws he gave articulation to the very quality in ourselves which is both the delight and the despair of our European friends, our centering of values in materiality and our high evaluation of what we call "know-how."

This national distrust of the past and of tradition, together with a sense of an obligation to use the average man rather than the hero as the protagonist of our works, results in the distrust of literary forms and the impatience with plot and structure which led the realist to demand not the symmetry of plot but the asymmetry of life in serious works of fiction. The distrust of ritual, which for a while stripped the American meeting house of decoration and removed from American Protestantism most of the vestiges of ritual; the distrust of ceremony, which often stripped from the machinery of social intercourse the lubricant of cultivated manners—these distrusts are echoed in the plotless and often formless novel of the nineteenth-century realists.

Furthermore, the tendency to see the individual at the center of all significant experience, so that the most characteristic attitude of the century was called "rugged individualism" or "self-reliance," inevitably made the average man the measure of his nation and his national experience. When this happened, as Tocqueville had predicted, this man's mind and his passions, the impress of events upon him, the consequences for his emotions and his psyche of the actions in the world around him became the center of art. If, as I suspect is true, Henry James's *The Ambassadors* is the almost perfect realistic novel, one of the places where it is most realistic is in the fact that it is concerned in large measure with the impact of event upon the mind of Lambert Strether, its protagonist. It is not a far step from the early realist's admonitions to write truthfully from experience, to James's insistence that impressions and psychological states are the valid subject matter for the realist. Ultimately the realistic novel becomes phenomenalistic in its view of reality and in its technique; to be otherwise would be to betray its own basic tenets. Out of this phenomenalism comes its passionate concern with narrative point of view.

It is a truism about the American that the dark shadow of Puritanism lurks always behind his conscious actions. Our consciences have been present with great force in most of the actions of our lives. And nowhere does that conscience express itself more clearly than in the realist's sense that fiction should discharge responsibilities to its audiences, that it should be among the great truth speakers of the world, and that the truth it should be speaking is the truth of factual, demonstrable actuality. To distort for whatever reason is to falsify, and the Puritan conscience demands of the realist that he present the facts clearly, objectively, without argument, and allow these facts to speak for themselves. Hence the realistic novel employed the "scenic" or dramatic method, specialized in the unevaluated statement, was elaborately concerned with point of view—with how the actions came to be seen and told. And more often than not, the realist felt himself restricted from making explicit the judgment which he would pass on the observer or narrator of his story, with the result that we can never determine precisely how to take the narratives. A good example is James's famous ghost story, *The Turn of the Screw*, which, as many critics have pointed out, may be read as a straight ghost story with the governess as the heroine, or may be read as the record of psychotic hallucination, with the governess as the villainess. While I personally think James intended it to be open-ended (else why not close the framework?), the fact remains that the judgment of the true character of the governess cannot be made with confidence, for we simply do not see enough of her outside the story she tells to be certain.

Thus in subject matter and in technique realism subsumed the dominant tendencies of American life and aspirations in the last half of the nineteenth century. Early democrats like Cooper and Hawthorne who worked in the older romantic forms felt the inadequacy of the union of the American subject matter and the traditional literary genres and interpreted the disjunction as being the result of the weakness of America as a subject for artistic expression. But when, at last, the voice of the common man, the voice of the strident frontier, and the voices of spokesmen like Mark Twain, Howells, and James had shaped a vehicle for the expression of a Puritan, pragmatic, egalitarian society that still believed in progress and had little interest in the past, the resulting genre was the realistic novel. It was the embodiment of the American dream, the expression of the democratic hope, the articulation of the Protestant ethic.

While these dreams and hopes survived vigorously, the realistic novel flourished. When, in the closing years of the nineteenth century and the early years of the twentieth, a decay set in in these fundamental American beliefs, realism responded to that decay, first with the bitterness of the reform propaganda of the Muckraker novels, and then with the irony, the mocking cynicism, and the social satire of writers like Edith Wharton, Ellen Glasgow, Sinclair Lewis, John P. Marquand, and John

O'Hara. Other literary modes—naturalism, symbolism, expressionism, black comedy—have been more effective than realism as voices for our despair and our cosmic pessimism. Yet realism has remained, although diminished in the critical marketplace, still the conscience and the spokesman of the democratic dream and the democratic ideal. It is not the only important mode of American fiction, and it is no longer the dominant one, but it is truly there, and cannot be explained away by systems that distrust or dislike it.

"Of Everything the Unexplained and Irresponsible Specimen"

NOTES ON HOW TO READ AMERICAN REALISM

To write on how to read realistic writing is to invite the charges of being both ingenuous and arrogant. Yet it seems to me that much American realism is so often misread *on principle* today that the risk needs to be taken. As late as the 1890s the avant-garde in American literary circles was fighting for the right to represent the world as it literally was, as an end in itself; and against them was raised, in the pages of journals like *The Bookman* and by writers like F. Marion Crawford, the charge that literature should not reflect the tattletale gray of daily life but should present man in ideal and/or entertaining postures. In the past eighty years, however, the wheel has come full circle. Today our critics seek for archetypal patterns, or recurrent symbols, or a structure of images, or an order of meaning which transcends the actual, or a conscious distortion of the actual in order to present some higher or extraterrestrial truth. A writer who attempts to communicate directly, clearly, and unmistakably the literal experience of an actual world in a specific time and place, a writer who can say, *mutatis mutandis*, with Fra Lippo Lippi:

> . . . we're made so that we love
> First when we see them painted, things we have passed
> Perhaps a hundred times nor cared to see;
> And so they are better, painted—better to us,
> Which is the same thing. Art was given for that—

such a writer receives short and often sneering shrift among many present-day critics. Fra Lippo's Prior admonished him,

> Your business is not to catch men . . .
> With homage to the perishable clay . . .
> Your business is to paint the souls of men—

and, assuming the accuracy of Browning's portrait, that just goes to show that critics have changed remarkably little since the fifteenth century!

But realists whose works have an appeal for contemporary critics, despite their methods, are often simply translated from their own mode into the mode which the critic fancies. Such a writer if he reads his critics may discover that he has invented symbols of which he never dreamed and constructed meanings of which he was utterly unaware. He may shudderingly recall that Edmund Wilson once remarked, with a straight face, "One is led to conclude that, in *The Turn of the Screw*, not merely is the governess self-deceived, but that James is self-deceived about her." The issue, of course, is not that *The Turn of the Screw* lacks ambiguity, but that Wilson thinks James did not know it.

An allegory is done little violence when it is read as a work done in some other mode, for it will not yield a meaning when it is taken out of the essential frame in which it is cast. A work which rests on a conscious structure of symbols must be read in terms of those symbols or lose its quality as a work of art; its fundamental mode will not be misunderstood. Few people have failed to recognize that the basic mode of *Moby-Dick* is symbolic. Even the contemporary critics who rejected the work did so not because they did not perceive that it was symbolic, but because they thought that its symbolism constructed an insane world. A novel like *The Scarlet Letter*, despite the intensity with which it explores the character of Hester Prynne, forces us to see Hester, her actions, and the actions of the story as basically segments of a symbolic world that must be understood philosophically, and not as primarily a picture of a palpable actual. The praise which we justly lavish upon the novel comes out of our recognition of the skill with which Hawthorne has used its parts to create a symbolic whole that transcends the actuality of Puritan Boston and the adulteress Hester.

Realism, however, does not contain this kind of built-in safeguard; that is, its adulation of the technique of the self-effaced author and its attempt to present the actual conspire to make it essentially a report rather than a comment; therefore, the mythologizer can read it as myth; the symbolist can read it as symbol; the allegorist can read it as allegory; and the seeker after psychological meanings, such as Leslie Fiedler, can read it as love (of a sort) and death. For in an ideal sense, the mimetic artist brings before his reader a picture of the actual so clear, so exact, and so free from distortion that it exists for him as a segment of life itself and is subject, as life is, to a variety of interpretations. Such a statement cannot be made, even as a statement of an unattainable ideal, about symbolic, allegorical, or rhetorical writing.

Think for a moment about the criticism of *Moby-Dick*, where we may debate endlessly about the meaning of the white whale and its quest but never about the fundamental method by which that meaning is invested in the book, as opposed to the endless and conflicting interpretations of James's novel *The Ambassadors*, which is read as allegory (in the case of Mr. Quentin Anderson), as a satiric attack on the Puritan mind, as a romantic celebration of the Puritan mind, as a realistic picture of moral decay in Paris, as an idealistic celebration of aesthetic life in Paris, as a tragedy of man's lot in an evil world, as a comic novel, as an ironic novel, and, one is almost prompted to say, as any other kind of novel that the critic may think of at a given moment. Now, in a sense, James asked for just this confusion, because he freed his novel to a remarkable degree from the controls which tell the reader what to do—which give him explanations, directions, justifications, and apologiæ. If James's basic idea is adequately carried out, we perceive Paris and Mme de Vionnet as Strether does and make our—not James's—judgments of what the facts really are and what they mean. Of course James does not fully succeed in this objective—no one could—but he comes close, it seems to me. It is the nearness of James's approach here that makes *The Ambassadors* very close to the ideal realistic novel of its age.

The realists who dominated the literary scene in America between 1870 and 1900 and whose chief proponents were William Dean Howells and Henry James were self-conscious users of the actual, committed to the doctrine of presenting truthful types of common humanity, and presenting them without the intrusion of the author and with as nearly complete objectivity as they could achieve. Many aspects of the self-conscious theory of realism which these men expounded could be examined, but I should like to summarize a definition of the underlying concept which motivated this period in literary history on the Continent, in England, and in America, and then to examine briefly the characteristics which Howells and James each emphasized in the literary figure whom each insisted to have been his chief artistic model, the Russian novelist Ivan Turgenev.

René Wellek, in "Realism in Literary Scholarship," has defined the realism of the nineteenth century as "the objective representation of contemporary social reality." He also asserts, "It rejects the fantastic, the fairy-tale-like, the allegorical and the symbolic, the highly stylized, the purely abstract, and decorative. It means that we want no myth, no *Maerchen*, no world of dreams. It implies also a rejection of the improbable, of pure chance, and of extraordinary events, since reality is obviously conceived at that time, in spite of all local and personal differences, as the orderly world of nineteenth-century science, the world of cause and effect, a world without miracle, without transcendence, even if the individual may have preserved a personal religious faith." Professor Wellek adds that emphasis on *type* as the "all important association with objective social observation," was almost universal in realistic theory. He says, "in fiction the main technical demand of realist theory came to be impersonality, the complete absence of the author from his work, a suppression of any interference by the author. The theory had its main spokesman in Flaubert, but it was also a preoccupation of Henry James." This quality, which Joseph Warren Beach called "the self-effaced author," which Percy Lubbock made the central dogma of *The Craft of Fiction*, and which Wayne Booth, in *The Rhetoric of Fiction*, has brilliantly but not always sympathetically analyzed as "impersonal narration," is not only a technical strategy whose developing importance created the critical concept of point of view; it is also a basic philosophical position about the significance of the actual and the role of art.

Both James and Howells, despite their widely differing backgrounds and intellectual histories and the great differences in their subject matter, shared, as we have noted, a common literary master whose work and method each emulated through a large portion of his career, and whose artistic methods both carefully analyzed and praised in critical essays. This master was Ivan Turgenev. Howells said of the formative years of his literary career, "My most notable literary experience without doubt was the knowledge of Tourguénief's novels . . . Tourguénief's method is as far as art can go." In the latter part of his career, the example of Tolstoi's deep moral involvement in social problems led Howells to shift his ultimate allegiance to that Russian novelist; however, even then he believed that Tolstoi, "as an artistic worker," shared the qualities which he had earlier found in Turgenev, and his final greater appreciation of Tolstoi than of Turgenev was a judgment of what James might have called "the quality of their minds" and not of their arts.

Henry James, too, found in what he called the "beautiful genius" of Turgenev a literary model in the art of fiction and paid Turgenev the high compliment of imitating both his method and certain of his characters and situations in some of his novels, notably *Roderick Hudson*, *The American*, and *The Princess Casamassima*. In the Preface to *The Portrait of a Lady*, James credits, as his source for his method, Turgenev's theory of the "origin of the fictive picture," discusses in relation to Turgenev the subject of character as *disponibles*—a central concept in James's view of the novel at its best—and writes warmly of "The Admirable Russian," paying tribute to what he calls the "one much-embracing echo" of Turgenev. Oscar Cargill, in *The Novels of Henry James*, sees in the method James employed in *The Golden Bowl* "perhaps the most nearly ultimate and finest expression of the Turgenev method, in which . . . we know only what we discern from the action and the speech of the characters, whose revelation is our chief concern." James's essays on Turgenev are paeans of praise, sharply in contrast to the kinds of qualification that he makes in his critiques of writers like Balzac, Flaubert, Tolstoi, and Trollope. "No one," James declared, "has more of that sign of the born novelist" than Turgenev.

The primary quality which both Howells and James saw in Turgenev was the direct presentation of life with clarity, without interference, and through characters fully realized as people existing in their own right and for no other reason than that they were people. These characters were comprehended with such clarity and completeness that their common qualities were shared by all mankind and their special qualities were shared with their class; thus they became both types of man in general and types of their special social status, without their ever becoming symbols or allegorical figures. James expressed this idea very clearly when he wrote approvingly of Turgenev: "he has no recognition of unembodied ideas; an idea, with him, is such and such an individual, with such and such a nose and chin, such and such a hat and waistcoat, bearing the same relation to it as the look of a printed word does to its meaning." This must have been the quality in James himself which T.S. Eliot was referring to when he said that James had "a mind so fine that no idea could violate it."

Howells declared of Turgenev, "Here was a master who was apparently not trying to work out a plot, who was not even trying to work out a character, but was standing aside from the whole affair and letting the characters work the plot out." And he added, "It was not only that Tourguénief had painted life truly, but that he had painted it conscientiously." James was even more emphatic; he said: "Character, character expressed and exposed, is in all [Turgenev's works] what we inveterately find . . . the simplest account of him is to say that the mere play of it constitutes in every case his sufficient drama. No one has a closer vision, or a hand at once more ironic and more tender, for the individual figure. He sees it with its minutest signs and tricks—all its heredity of idiosyncrasies, all its particulars of weakness and strength, of ugliness and beauty, oddity and charm; yet it is of his essence that he sees in it the general flood

of life, steeped in its relations and contacts, struggling or submerged, a hurried particle in the stream. . . . He understands
so much that we almost wonder he can express anything; and
his expression is, indeed, wholly in absolute projection, in illustration, in giving of everything the unexplained and irresponsible specimen."

These statements of Howells and James about Turgenev remind us of the many similar remarks which other novelists have
made about the relationship of their materials to experience.
For example, F. Scott Fitzgerald in a letter to Maxwell Perkins
on July 30, 1934, defined his art as "the attempt . . . to recap-
ture the exact feel of a moment in time and space, exemplified
by people rather than by things . . . an attempt at a mature
memory of a deep experience." John P. Marquand, who worked
—I think with some distinction—in the realistic novel, in making one of his few critical judgments about fiction, said, "A
novel is great and good in direct proportion to the illusion it
gives of life and a sense of life. . . . [The reader] should feel
that he has been through an experience that may be as real . . .
[as] experiences in his own living . . . that he has walked with
living people." John O'Hara declared his intention as a novelist
to be "to record the way people talked and thought and felt, and
to do it with complete honesty and variety." James T. Farrell
once defined his method as the attempt to give "the precise con-
tent of life in environments described in [a particular] book."
And Henry James, in a letter to Robert Louis Stevenson, wrote:
"I want to leave a multitude of pictures of my time—so that the
number may constitute a total having a certain value as observation and testimony." Clearly this is a tradition of the novel
which places a high premium—perhaps the highest—on accurate portrayal of precisely observed people in social situations.

These writers have embraced a mimetic theory of art, one in
which the fidelity of the art object to its subject is its high crite-
rion. James declared, "The only reason for the existence of a
novel is that it does attempt to represent life. When it relin-
quishes this attempt . . . it will have arrived at a strange pass."
Howells asserted, "Realism is nothing more and nothing less

than the truthful treatment of material." And he defined this truthful treatment of material as the attempt "to report the phrase and carriage of every-day life. . . . to tell just how [the author] has heard men talk and seen them look." Throughout his long career as field-general and spokesman for American realism Howells insisted upon the presentation of the commonplace, in his own phraseology "the simple, the natural, and the honest." And he believed that the best method by which this honestly viewed and directly expressed picture of the actual could be presented to the reader was that which Turgenev had practiced with great distinction. Howells said that Turgenev's "fiction is to the last degree dramatic. The persons are sparsely described, and briefly accounted for, and then they are left to transact their affair, whatever it is, with the least possible comment or explanation from the author. The effect flows naturally from their characters, and when they have done or said a thing you conjecture why as unerringly as you would if they were people whom you knew outside a book." Howells, who praised Tolstoi beyond measure, could still condemn him for his "didactic" stories which, he declared, "dwindled into allegories . . . Where Tolstoi becomes impatient of his office of artist, and prefers to be directly a teacher, he robs himself of more than half his strength." To show what he means, Howells adds in the same essay that Tolstoi's great quality is his "transparency of style, unclouded by any mist of the personality which we mistakenly value in style, and which ought no more be there than the artist's personality should be in a portrait." And he condemns the *Kreutzer Sonata* as "terrible" because its author "descended to exegesis." It is also worthy of note that both James and Howells thought Hawthorne's most socially oriented novel, *The Blithedale Romance*, to be his best work; and both considered *The Scarlet Letter* to be flawed by its symbolism and its tendency toward allegory.

The point that I am trying to make—a very simple one, indeed—is that there has been, and still is, a significant movement in American fiction which values very highly the artist's ability to reproduce actuality as a sufficient and admirable end in itself.

For some, like Howells, this actuality is largely social and direct. For some, like James, profound epistemological questions raise their heads, and the ability of the artist to know the actual comes under serious question. Yet even James, who virtually invented the psychological novel in his explorations of the accuracy of our reports of the real, in moving into psychological issues enriched but did not abandon the mimetic obligation of the novelist. In his best-known critical essay, "The Art of Fiction," he defines the imagination in mimetic—almost classical—terms, calling it "the power to guess the unseen from the seen, to trace the implications of things, to judge the whole piece by the pattern, the condition of feeling life in general so completely that you are well on your way to knowing any particular corner of it." And he gave in the same essay a magnificent definition of psychological experience as "an immense sensibility, a kind of huge spiderweb of the finest silken threads suspended in the chamber of consciousness, and catching every air-borne particle in its tissue. It is the very atmosphere of the mind; and when the mind is imaginative . . . it takes to itself the faintest hints of life, it converts the very pulses of the air into revelations."

When the realist concentrates, not on symbols or allegories but on

> The beauty and the wonder and the power,
> The shapes of things, their colours, lights and shades,
> Changes, surprises—,

when the realist succeeds in achieving this goal of mimesis, he presents us with a picture of complex experience which we are to see and respond to as a segment of life. We may demand of art other things than this—indeed, many of us do—we may feel that such lowly aims are too earth-bound for our admiration. But when we read writers themselves committed to such aims, we should be willing to take them on their terms, and not re-write them into ours in our critical essays. As Northrop Frye lamented in the 1962 English Lecture at Harvard, "we tend to make naive judgments on literature which assume that literary works form a kind of continuous allegorical commentary." Leon

25

Edel has commented on what he calls "the bizarre critical image of Henry James," saying that critics have called him a "tragic visionary," a "melodramatist," a "religious visionary," an "allegorist," a "realist," and a "naturalist." And at least one critic has found in sedate William Dean Howells significant phallic symbols! Clearly it is time to start looking at realistic novelists in their own terms.

James expressed those terms well when in writing of his master Ivan Turgenev's handling of character, he praised his superiority "to the strange and second-rate policy of explaining or presenting them by reprobation or apology—of taking the short cuts and anticipating the emotions and judgments about them that should be left, at best, to the perhaps not most intelligent reader." He saw Turgenev's value, as I would have you see the value of James and the other realists, as "absolute projection," as "giving of everything the unexplained and irresponsible specimen."

Detached Laughter in the South

I have found that any fiction that comes out of the South is going to be called grotesque by the Northern reader—unless it is grotesque, in which case it's going to be called realism,"[1] declared Flannery O'Connor, who also asserted that "the woods are full of regional writers and it is the great horror of every serious southern writer that he will become one."[2] Thus, in her wry way, she marked off a body of writing uniquely associated with the southeastern region of the United States, asserted that it had differences deeper than the local-color qualities of a section of the nation, and expressed her stubborn pride in those differences.

The average reasonably well-informed northern reader may want to debate Miss O'Connor's definition of realism, but he will certainly agree that southern writing in this century has been different. Even if he shares the arch provincialism of New York City that led Richard Gilman recently to say, "The time is long past when southern writers were either at the center of American literature or powerful influences on the flank,"[3] when you say "southern writing" to this average northern reader, he thinks he knows what to expect. It is the Gothic, revelling deliciously and lasciviously in its horrors. It is the historical, restoring past glories now gone with the wind. It is the idealized and the sentimental, so sickly sweet that he feels as though he had swallowed *Love Story* at one gulp. It is the grotesque, depraved, and deformed. Occasionally, too, it is the indignant and the socially aware. But this northern reader seldom gets from the words "southern writing" a picture that has a substantial comic dimension, and this is surprising, because for the last one hundred and fifty years the comic has been a major, though often ignored, segment of the southern literary imagination.

27

Miss O'Connor has other surprises for this northern reader, for while acknowledging the label of grotesque for her characters, she disavows its applicability and asserts a realistic intention. And if her northern reader means by grotesque—a southern characteristic which he does recognize and expect—the currently fashionable meaning of the term, he is likely to see it as "an outgrowth of contemporary interest in the irrational, distrust of any cosmic order, frustration at man's lot in the universe,"[4] an element of "black humor," when it is comic, a form of distortion whose purpose is expressionistic, not representative. If Miss O'Connor is correct, then what he sees as grotesque and expressionistic in southern writing is something quite different.

To understand that difference, it is necessary here, as it is with many things southern, to go back for a moment into the past. For to a degree unthinkable for any other section of a nation with a history as short as that of the United States, the South has preserved and cherished its temporal continuities. In a time of discontinuities, the South has revered tradition and community. In a world that, by and large, pants passionately after the new and the untried, it has adapted the received and the known to the needs of the present and the future. Nowhere is this essentially conservative attitude more clearly expressed than in its literature where it reverences history, Gothicism, sentimentality, and formalist criticism—the primary modes of its writers in the nineteenth century. That this traditionalism is also true of its comic writing should be no surprise, for the irreverent but conservative muse of comedy is the muse of limitations, of restraints, of tradition, the portrayer of human limitations and frailties rather than superhuman aspirations and ideals—at least so it has often been, and so it is in the American South. Hence, to look at humor in the recent South it is necessary to see it as a continuation of traditional comic writing in the region, even though the South has frequently been viewed as though it were an arena exclusively dedicated to tragedy or cruel exploitation or sickeningly pious sentiment. What has comedy, committed as she is to mocking the discrepancies between appearance and reality, to do with so self-deluding a region as the South? many will ask. But such a view is peculiarly unhistorical, for few would deny the ribald life and triumphant vigor of that group of nineteenth-century writers whom we call the humorists of the Old Southwest, and only those whose sense of history is too weak to instruct them in the chronological course of the westward moving frontier in the first half of the nineteenth century will fail to see that that flood of writing was produced in Georgia, Mississippi, and Alabama—in what was the southwestern frontier in the period before the Civil War. Augustus Baldwin Longstreet's *Georgia Scenes* (1835) is the comic portrayal of a backwoods culture in Georgia in the first third of the nineteenth century. Joseph Glover Baldwin's *The Flush Times of Alabama and Mississippi* (1853) is an amusing record of the rascality, ignorance, and depravity of life on that wild and roaring frontier. Johnson Jones Hooper's *Some Adventures of Captain Simon Suggs* (1845) follows a rascal's wild, picaresque adventures on that frontier. George Washington Harris's sketches about Sut Lovingood, an exuberant and uninhibited denizen of Tennessee, were collected as *Sut Lovingood Yarns* (1867). And there are many others, most notably Thomas Bangs Thorpe, whose *Big Bear of Arkansas* is almost the archetype of a brand of humor resting upon dialect and tall tale and comic character. It was a rich strain of earthy humor which these writers—mostly lawyers, politicians, and journalists—produced as an avocation on the Old Southwestern frontier.[5]

These early southern humorists have a number of common characteristics. The writer, either in his own person or through a narrative persona, usually belongs to a social class quite different from and superior to that of the frontier wild life which he describes, and he remains consistently the outsider and the observer who brings to bear upon the subjects of his portrayal a set of standards, a level of culture, and a facility with language quite out of keeping with the subjects being described. Each of these narrators depends upon this social and cultural distance to make possible the representation of crudities, cruelties, and depravities that would otherwise have been shocking almost beyond the bearing to the reader to whom the work is addressed.

The mode in which these writers worked was neither Gothic nor sentimental. It was detached, cool, amused, generally tolerant, and often sardonic. Theirs were reports to a society back home on what was happening on the wild frontier, but these reports became historical only after the westward movement had passed the region by and had left them as records of the past. The primary method which these writers employed was that of the realistic portrayal of an extravagant and wild life done with great exuberance and a peculiar delight in the vitality and the strangeness of idiomatic speech on the southwestern frontier. Tall tales were sometimes told; indeed, they were one of the hallmarks of this kind of humor, and folk heroes paraded their might across the pages of these books—men like Davy Crockett and Mike Fink. The primary method, however, was literal reporting of the strange and wonderful doings of the natives, colored by a certain amount of amused extravagance, in reports sent back home to an urbane and civilized society about the antics of the natives.

This was not the only form of humor in the South during the nineteenth century. George Bagby wrote wittily and comically in the *Southern Literary Messenger,* and others imitated the quiet wit of the English periodical essays, but the uniquely southern form of humor dealt with this frontier. Humor was the device relied on to make the portrayal of this coarse, rough life palatable and enjoyable rather than horrifying and sickening, for it could easily have been a subject for Gothic treatment. For example, William Gilmore Simms worked essentially in the Gothic tradition in many of his novels, and in his attempts to portray in 1835 and 1836 the Loyalist forces during the American Revolution, he piled up the terrors to which they were submitted in the early days of the conflict by their Whig adversaries and the horrors which they later perpetrated in revenge, making themselves into creatures of terror, drinkers of blood, frightening outlaws. However, by the middle 1850s, Simms had virtually abandoned the Gothic approach, and in his last two Revolutionary novels, *The Forayers* (1855) and *Eutaw* (1856), he shifted to the comic portrayal of these depraved people creating a great host of far from lovable but certainly laughable and impressive rascals and ruffians who represented the Tory forces. Thus comedy for him became an effective medium for downgrading the seriousness of hated causes and for attacking the character of those he disliked.[6]

In this century, the South has produced essentially two kinds of humor not greatly different in kind from that of Bagby and that of the Southwest humorists. Associated with the Tidewater and the South Carolina Low Country was an urbane and polished form of writing practiced by James Branch Cabell and Ellen Glasgow in Virginia and by Robert Molloy and Josephine Pinckney around Charleston. This humor is essentially that of the novel of manners or of urbane fantasy. Charming and witty, it exists only because the Virginia Tidewater and the Carolina Low Country represented at the time that these people were writing one of the few sections of America that had a code of manners sufficiently firm to enable the comedy of manners to be constructed around it. Perhaps the finest writing in this tradition done by any southerner was by Ellen Glasgow in her Queenborough trilogy, *The Romantic Comedians* (1926), *They Stooped to Folly* (1929), and *The Sheltered Life* (1932).[7]

But opposed to this kind of polished and witty humor there has also existed in the South a raucous, ribald, and extravagant humor which is the realist's way of dealing with the unbearable or the intolerable aspects of life without shifting into the tradition of the Gothic or the tragic. It is a kind of humor that depends, as had that of the Old Southwest, upon the distance in social class and learning between the putative narrator and the subject in order to make bearable what might otherwise have been unbearable to the reader. It has its roots in aspects of the social condition which constitute affronts to human dignity and arouse the deepest and most penetrating anger, or in cosmic conditions that dwarf and stunt human beings, but it controls and shapes these affronts, this anger, or this vision by establishing a redeeming comic distance.

To attempt to deal with the humor of William Faulkner is a task for a book, not a section of an essay, and I shall use him not as a subject for analysis but as an object to point to before going on to my two representative writers. William Faulkner can be considered the "compleat" southern writer, for he has demonstrated with a high degree of artistry and accomplishment almost every mode of southern fiction which exists in this century. He dealt with Gothic horrors and extravagances in *Sanctuary* (1931). He carried the historical novel to its highest limits of artistic success in *Absalom, Absalom!* (1936). He made art out of the idealized and sentimentalized view of the Civil War in *The Unvanquished* (1938). He dealt with the peculiar mixture of symbolism and naturalism that we associate with the South in *Light in August* (1932) and *The Sound and the Fury* (1929), and in the Snopes trilogy—*The Hamlet* (l940), *The Town* (1957), and *The Mansion* (1960)—he carried realistic comedy working in the tradition of the frontier humorist to its highest accomplishment in this century. Those who call *The Hamlet* the finest comic novel produced by a southern American certainly can feel some confidence in their judgment. It is worth noting that *The Hamlet* is in four parts, that Parts I and IV deal with the comic theme of barter, and that Parts II and III deal with the other major theme of the novel, love.[8] Thus the serious elements of the novel are enclosed by the comic. This use of the comic tone to restore an equitable world is not unusual for Faulkner; the opening and concluding chapters of *Light in August*, dealing with Lena Grove, serve a similar although more restricted function of setting the tragic horrors of the main portion of that novel in a perspective against a comic pastoral.[9] But the Snopes trilogy is loaded throughout with scenes of extravagant humor. The Snopeses themselves are thoroughly in keeping with the natives of the southwestern frontier of Longstreet and Baldwin, and there may be a close relationship between Flem Snopes, the leader of the Snopes clan, and Johnson Jones Hooper's Simon Suggs. The Snopeses represent the lowest class. They swarm over the land, almost seeming to crawl from under stones and rotten logs, and gradually take possession of it. Under the coldly acquisitive leadership of Flem Snopes they move from Frenchman's Bend, a small country community, into the town, and finally to the triumphant possession of the once glorious South. *The Hamlet* is a loosely linked series of episodes about the Snopeses and their way of life, breaking into separate episodes. Some of those episodes, first published as short stories and episodes in other of the Yoknapatawpha novels, represent an almost pure survival of the characters, actions, and mode of southwestern humor, even to being recounted by a narrator, V.K. Ratliff, from a position of superior knowledge. Such a one is the story of how Ab Snopes was bested in a horse trade by Pat Stamper, a horse swap story of a sort that goes back to Longstreet's *Georgia Scenes*.[10] Perhaps the funniest story that Faulkner ever wrote, "Spotted Horses," appears as an episode in *The Hamlet*. It recounts the events that befell Frenchman's Bend when Flem Snopes brought in a band of wild, untamable Texas horses and sold them to the men of the community.[11] That novel closes with a tale of the "salting" of treasure in the old Frenchman's place in Flem's efforts to sell it to Ratliff. In *The Mansion*, generally a novel quite inferior to *The Hamlet*, there are redeeming pieces of comic delight, such as the episode when Byron Snopes sends his four wild and uncivilized children to visit kinsmen in Jefferson and they almost burn Clarence Snopes at the stake, and the incident when Clarence, running for Congressman, is making a speech and Ratliff has two boys brush Snopes's trousers with bush branches saturated with dog urine, so that the dogs line up to lift their legs to his trouser legs while he is speaking. He is eliminated from the race on the grounds that the district shouldn't be represented by a man that every "dog that happens by can't tell from a fence post." In *The Hamlet* there is the tall tale of Flem Snopes outwitting the Devil in Hell and gaining ownership of the infernal regions.

All these episodes and many others like them, almost traditional in the long southwestern humor material, Faulkner uses to fashion a picture of his mythical county, firmly embedded in specific people and actions and described with great intensity. Throughout this picture of what the South had fallen to and of those who controlled it in the years between the end of the Civil War and the beginning of the First World War, Faulkner used humor to allow him to describe these people and their way of life without treating them either with the Gothic horrors which they might have inspired or the sentimental sympathy which we might have had for them had they been presented as the culturally deprived. Neither Faulkner nor his reader regards the bulk of the characters in the Snopes trilogy as on his own cultural level. The things which happen to them are seen as comic rather than terrifying. Humor was among the major means by which Faulkner described his world with accuracy and set it apart from the mainstream while not denying its actuality. When, as happens in *The Mansion*, Faulkner loses the distance which allows him to look without involvement at these characters, when he begins to move in close and understand Flem Snopes, and when he begins to follow Mink Snopes's determination to leave prison and seek revenge upon Flem with some admiration for his determination and persistence—at this point the comedy begins to weaken and the trilogy begins to weaken as well. There is in Faulkner's Snopes trilogy vastly more than merely a redoing of the humor of the Old Southwest, but that kind of humor is one significant, important, and very happy element in the novels. Faulkner could be—and at his best he was —truly a master of the comic mode of storytelling, and he used that mode as a means of permitting the realistic portrayal of characters and actions that might otherwise have overwhelmed us with their crudeness or with their horror, as a means of achieving distance, perspective, and the redemption of detachment.

Certainly this treatment of Faulkner's Snopes trilogy is very incomplete, but I hope that it is sufficient to suggest to those familiar with his work that Faulkner consciously worked from time to time in the generally detached mode of the humorists of the Old Southwest frontier, the detached mode which I am maintaining is the most typical method of the writers of humor in the South. Such distance is always bought with a price and for a purpose. In Faulkner's case the price is the lowering of his dark tragic intensity; the purpose is the presentation of frail or ignorant or even rapacious people without converting them into devils. For example, Thomas Sutpen, in *Absalom, Absalom!*,

looms vast and demonic over a blasted and monumental landscape, in large part because we see him through the eyes of
those who are deeply involved with his tragic and demonic implications. Had V.K. Ratliff told the Sutpen story one of the
things that would have happened to Sutpen would have been a
great scaling down of his superhuman magnitude, and Wash
Jones, who kills him with a scythe, would have appeared not as
a fated Fury wielding the knife of time, but a shambling poor
white with a rusty blade. Comedy is the right mode for the realistic portrayal of people seen in terms of their weaknesses and
limitations, particularly if one wants to portray their twisted
selves without converting them into creatures of horror.

Two other southern writers with whom I shall deal belong in
this tradition of detached comedy, Erskine Caldwell and Flannery O'Connor. Both have produced distinctively humorous
bodies of material, though in the minds of many readers neither
should be thought of as a comic writer, and the differences in
their visions of the world are so great that, at first glance, they
seem to share nothing except a landscape and a tendency to
draw grotesque characters. Erskine Caldwell was overcome
with the evil which grew out of the economic and agricultural
deprivations that were associated with the South he grew up in.
Flannery O'Connor writes of the poor whites and the middle
class in middle Georgia and Tennessee, the same people with
whom Caldwell deals. But, being a profoundly religious person, she sees them under the light of eternity, and is deeply concerned with the spiritual deprivations which they suffer from
their unsatisfied hunger for God.

Perhaps the principal inheritor and to some extent exploiter
of the frontier tradition in southern literature is Erskine Caldwell, whose world is largely populated by people that would
have been thoroughly familiar to Johnson Jones Hooper,
George Washington Harris, and Augustus Baldwin Longstreet.
Indeed, since most of Caldwell's best work is centered in and
around Augusta, Georgia, the locale of Longstreet's *Georgia
Scenes*, to set Caldwell's portrayal against Longstreet's is to see
what has happened to the same kinds of people under the im-

pact of economic poverty, spiritual decay, and the collapse of the agricultural system. If there was about Longstreet's Georgia denizens an enormous zest and vigor, there is about the inhabitants of *Tobacco Road, God's Little Acre,* and *Trouble in July* a debilitation and weakness in which only hunger and sex remain forces that inspire any vigorous action. In this drab world in which repetition becomes the dominant tone—the characters repeat endlessly the same actions, an aspect of *Tobacco Road,* for example, which the stage version caught very well by an almost stylized reiteration of characters and actions —these people are portrayed at the most elementary level possible. They are reduced to the level and the actions of animals. Social decorum is totally removed; public and private made interchangeable, and stimulus and response automatic.

But Caldwell, in presenting these characters, differs significantly from the kind of exuberant extravagance which had characterized the southwestern humorists. Where they had sought for unusual and spectacular events, he uses seemingly endless repetition. Where they had used an extravagant style, capitalizing upon the rhetorical excessiveness of southern speech and southern action, he uses a plain, powerful, and direct style. Where they had portrayed the positive actions of their characters, Caldwell's people exist in the mental state of refusal. As Kenneth Burke pointed out in a brilliant essay on Caldwell, he "puts people into complex social situations while making them act with the scant, crude, tropisms of an insect."[12] Certainly Caldwell's characters on one level should precipitate in his reader a sense of horror and of shock, a revulsion at the skill with which he exploits their animal nature. Yet it is actually difficult to read of his characters in wildly incongruous situations stripped to the animal level without finding in them the ludicrous and the ridiculous, rather than the terrifying. It has been customary to think of Caldwell as having produced in the very early 1930s a few important novels—*Tobacco Road, God's Little Acre, Journeyman,* and *Trouble in July*—and a group of short stories of great distinction, including "Kneel to the Rising Sun" and "Country Full of Swedes," and then having passed into a period of hackwork and conscious pornography which renders him no longer a serious figure. Probably this view will be corrected with the passage of time as James Korges has asserted with great vigor in his *Erskine Caldwell.*[13] Whether Korges is correct or not, it is true that the comic strain present in the early novels is still very active in the ones that he has written since the early 1950s, a number of which compare very favorably with his earlier. Perhaps his funniest novel is *God's Little Acre* (1933), possibly his most satisfactory is *Trouble in July* (1940), and *Georgia Boy* (1943) is his finest nostalgic picture of childhood. But *Claudelle Inglis* (1968) is an almost flawless sexual comedy with the skill of storytelling and the exuberance of a Chaucerian fabliau; *Miss Mama Aimee* (1967) is possibly his best novel since *Georgia Boy*, and *Summertime Island* (1968) is a treatment of a boy's initiation only a small degree lesser than his best work.

Miss Mama Aimee is based upon a whole series of comic reversals and contains some marvelous characters, such as the preacher Raley Purdy, who, when he sees a girl unclothed, worries about what Billy Graham would think if he saw him in such a situation. The girl asks, "Who's Billy Graham?" and Purdy replies, "I can't talk about Billy Graham when you're stark naked—he wouldn't want me to."[14]

At the heart of Caldwell's portrayal of his world is a sense of what the social system can do—indeed, has done—to people, and upon that basis he makes his strongest claims. In his autobiography Caldwell says of *Tobacco Road*, "I felt that I would never be able to write successfully about other people in other places until first I had written the story of the landless and poverty-stricken families living on East Georgia sand hills and tobacco roads. . . . I wanted to tell the story of the people I knew in the manner in which they actually lived their lives . . . and to tell it without regard for fashions in writing and traditional plots."[15] In that novel which contained the essence of most of what he was to do best down to the present, Caldwell wrote with great simplicity and force of style, a clear, hard, clean, and forceful prose, describing people whose lives are so stripped of economic and social hope that they become grotesque parodies of human beings twisted by the simplest hungers, totally lacking in dignity and in integrity. "All I wanted to do," Caldwell said, "was simply to describe to the best of my ability the aspirations and despair of the people I wrote about."[16]

Caldwell's people are twisted and misshaped by social and economic deprivation, by the exhausting of the soil, by a cruel tenant farmer system, by the absence of the most elementary aspects of culture. Tobacco Road and its environment is a soil depleted, a people washed out and drained and responding like animals to the forces around them, yet Caldwell seems to be saying, "Fertilize the soil, return the price of cotton to a subsistence level, give them opportunity, and hope will follow, and in another generation something like the good life may return." The system is wrong, but the system, he believes, is remedial. Hence, he can feel a social anger, and he can portray through telling reductions to the animal the character of life and the quality of existence in this kind of world. But he knows that these characters, however misshaped, are people, and they are people upon whom he lavishes much of his warmest attention. "It seemed to me that the most authentic and enduring materials of fiction were the people themselves,"[17] he said. And he believes that to represent such people you need to be able to deal with them realistically on one level and yet without contempt while you describe the system which makes them what they are. This is a difficult strategy and one for which Caldwell adapted successfully the methods and the uses of the comic.

The world these people inhabit is one of cruel limitations and deprivations that twist and distort. To have portrayed the products of such deprivation as monsters would have been to misrepresent their human qualities, but to portray them as other than distorted and grotesque would have been to ignore the lesson of what a cruel economic system does to those under it. Comedy is the obvious answer; for comedy is the mode of limitations; comedy is the mode of hope; but above all, comedy gives the distance between reader and subject that allows grotesqueries to be seen with objectivity.

In recent years the southern writer most frequently discussed as a creator of grotesques has been Flannery O'Connor, for a great deal of attention has been given to her portraits of southern poor whites in middle Georgia and Tennessee, and the key to her comic mode has often been sought. It seems to me that she is solidly in the tradition of southern detached humor, but there is a crucial difference between her and most of her fellow southern writers, both past and present, a difference which accounts for the special kind and quality of her comedy. She was a Catholic writer in a Protestant world, and she saw the writing of fiction as a Christian vocation. She declared, "I see from the standpoint of Christian orthodoxy. This means that for me the meaning of life is centered in our Redemption by Christ and what I see in the world I see in relation to that."[18] What gives distance and comic perspective to her view of the world is fundamentally a religious distancing resulting from her confidence of her own salvation in a world of those futilely seeking for surety. As St. Augustine said, "Our souls are restless till they find rest in Thee." The world she portrays is a world made up of such restless, seeking souls, primitive in mind, Protestant in religion, sharing a deep common and personal awareness of the awful and the awesome presence and power of God in the world but a power and a presence which they can recognize but which they do not accept. Living in a world not ordered to an adequate sense of this power and presence of God, these characters seek to deny Him or to pervert their hunger for Him, and thus they become grotesque and unnatural. It is from the perspective of one who has found peace and rests secure in the knowledge of herself that Miss O'Connor can look out with a kind of amused pity upon a world that is still troubled and seeking, though it knows it not, salvation from its godlessness.

This perspective, though it is religious and philosophical, is not greatly different in its aesthetic effect from the distance of class or political position or economic status which has been for a hundred and fifty years essential to the functioning of the kind of realistic humor fundamental to the South. And this assurance of hers, this sense that the ultimate reality transcends the physical world which she portrays with directness and hard clarity makes all that happens within that world for Flannery O'Connor important only in what can come after it. Hence, there occurs repeatedly in her work those moments when not merely the humiliation of the flesh but the destruction of physical life proves to be an open door to a spiritual victory. People die in her stories with grace given them in their moments of expiration, as though death were to her a triumph.

This perspective gives her an enormous freedom, and it is a freedom which she consciously exercises as a comic writer. Of her novel *Wise Blood* she said, "The book was written with zest and, if possible, it should be read that way. It is a comic novel about the Christian *malgré lui*, and as such, very serious, for all comic novels that are any good must be about matters of life and death."[19] This kind of comedy, in one sense close to that which gives its title to Dante's great work, is a function of a tone which finds its basis in her own religious security, as Martha Stephens has persuasively pointed out.[20]

In the world of her fiction, Flannery O'Connor has dealt extensively with tortured, tormented, and distorted people and treated them both with comic detachment and with sympathy. The peculiar mixture of detachment and sympathy which Miss O'Connor achieves approaches being unique in American writing. She herself suggested, "Whenever I am asked why southern writers particularly have a penchant for writing about freaks, I say it is because we are still able to recognize one. To be able to recognize a freak you have to have some conception of the whole man, and in the South the general conception of man is still in the main theological."[21] These "freaks" are such because they are far from whole.

As a writer of comedy Miss O'Connor is best in the short story, and her most successful efforts here are in such stories as "Good Country People" and "The Life You Save May Be Your Own" in her first volume of short stories. Her method is exemplified very well in the story "Good Country People." This is the story of Joy Hopewell, the daughter of a widow Mrs. Hopewell, who regards herself as considerably above the simple people whom she sees about her and whom she calls "good country people." Joy, who changes her name to Hulga to spite her mother and who has an artificial leg, having had one of her legs shot off when she was a child, is thirty-two years old, has a Ph.D. in philosophy, suffers from a bad heart condition, and is living at home. She is an atheist, and proudly declares that she believes in nothing. A young Bible salesman—clearly from "good country people"—visits them and Hulga sets out to seduce him into atheism. She leads him to the hayloft in the barn and there discovers that he is far from "good country people"— that instead, one of his Bibles has been hollowed out and contains a bottle of whiskey, a set of cards with pornographic pictures on the back, and a package of contraceptives. He steals her glasses, removes her artificial leg, and takes it with him, and leaves her alone, in the hayloft without her leg, declaring to her as he leaves, "Hulga you ain't so smart. I been believing in nothing ever since I was born!"[22] The story is shocking and amusing, and its amusement comes from the fact that Hulga has found in the young Bible salesman precisely what she has sought all her life, and it has betrayed her and left her without the means to move or to see.

On one level this story is a parable of the nihilism of atheism, but on another level, it is a comic masterpiece. What makes it a comic masterpiece is, as much as anything else, the dry, wry, hard, and sardonic quality of Flannery O'Connor's style. A few examples from the story will illustrate: "Mrs. Hopewell had no bad qualities of her own but she was able to use other people's in such a constructive way that she never felt the lack."[23] "The large hulking Joy, whose constant outrage had obliterated every expression from her face, would stare just a little to the side of her, her eyes icy blue, with the look of someone who had achieved blindness by an act of will and means to keep it."[24] "The girl had taken the Ph.D. in philosophy and this left Mrs. Hopewell at a complete loss. You could say, 'My daughter is a nurse,' or 'My daughter is a school teacher,' or even 'My daughter is a chemical engineer.' You could not say, 'My daughter is a philosopher.'"[25] "As a child she had sometimes been subject to feelings of shame, but education had removed the last traces of that as a good surgeon scrapes for cancer; she would no more have felt it over what he was asking than she would have believed in his Bible. But she was as sensitive about the artificial leg as a peacock about his tail."[26]

Miss O'Connor is aware of the caste structures that a relatively fixed social order can produce and that have fascinated many other southern writers. For example, in a very late story, "Revelation," she says:

> Sometimes Mrs. Turpin occupied herself at night naming the classes of people. On the bottom of the heap were most colored people, not the kind she would have been if she had been one, but most of them; then next to them—not above, just away from—were the white trash; then above them were the home-owners, and above them the home-and-land owners, to which she and Claud belonged. Above she and Claud were people with a lot of money and much bigger houses and much more land. But here the complexity of it would begin to bear in on her, for some of the people with a lot of money were common and ought to be below she and Claud and some of the people who had good blood had lost their money and had to rent and then there were colored people who owned their homes and land as well. There was a colored dentist in town who had two red Lincolns and a swimming pool and a farm with registered white-face cattle on it.[27]

These qualities of knowledge, sharp perception, and comic distance are mixed in all her work with great zest and a stylistic precision so exact as to be almost overwhelming. Her combination of religious attitude and sardonic voice give vivid pictures of her world shaped by her personal angle of vision. In the early stories, those collected in *A Good Man Is Hard to Find*,[28] the delight she takes in her "freaks" is greatest, although it is present in large degree in *Wise Blood*,[29] a novel and her first published book. But *Wise Blood*, like *The Hamlet* at least in this respect, was a novel parts of which had originally been written as her earliest short stories.[30] As Miss O'Connor matured as a writer— she was only twenty years old when she submitted her first published story[31]—her themes deepened and her view of the world, although never losing its comic detachment, took on a more somber quality. In "Everything That Rises Must Converge," first published in 1961,[32] her sardonic portrait of Julian, the self-deceiving college graduate, is devastating, but the death of his mother does not have the comic distance which she had magnificently achieved in "A Good Man Is Hard to Find." "Parker's Back," posthumously published,[33] is a hilarious situation, but its theological meaning is impressed unmistakably on it with a hand heavier than usual.

But in these later stories and in the second novel, *The Violent Bear It Away* (1960), the basic comic method does not change; although the seriousness of her intention deepens, she does not depart from the accuracy of her portrayal of the literal world. Elizabeth Bishop properly observed of Miss O'Connor's books, "They are clear, hard, vivid, and full of bits of description, phrases, and an odd insight. . . . Critics who accuse her of exaggeration are quite wrong, I think. I lived in Florida for several years next to a flourishing 'Church of God'. . . . After [this] nothing Flannery O'Connor ever wrote could seem at all exaggerated to me."[34] I have argued elsewhere that her portrayal of the southern region is accurate,[35] and I have asserted that "within two blocks of the Regency Hyatt [in Atlanta] you can find street evangelists extolling their primitive religions in tone and manner that make you think Hazel Motes of *Wise Blood* has come back to life."[36]

Miss O'Connor's succinct, witty, and very direct prose is used with great success in picturing her segment of the South as a microcosm of the human lot. She wanted, as Hawthorne had, to produce fiction "that should evolve some deep lesson and should possess physical substance enough to stand alone."[37] The vision she had of man was not of a cloud-scraping demigod, a wielder of vast powers, but of a frail, weak creature, imperfect and incomplete in all his parts. To body forth such a vision calls for either comedy or pathos, and pathos was alien to Flannery O'Connor's nature and her beliefs.

Erskine Caldwell and Flannery O'Connor were the inheritors of a long southern tradition of detached humor, and they employed it on the same kinds of people in many of the same locales, but for radically different purposes. Both sought salvation for the denizens of their worlds. In Caldwell's case, as Kenneth Burke observed, "In so far as he is moved by the need of salvation, he seems minded to find it in the alignments of political exhortation, by striving mainly to see that we and he take the right side on matters of social justice."[38] Flannery O'Connor, too, was seeking salvation, but the salvation she sought was transcendent; it was to be found only in God. She once said:

> The problem for [a Southern] novelist will be to know how far he can distort without destroying, and in order not to destroy, he will have to descend far enough into himself to reach those underground springs that give life to his work. This descent into himself will, at the same time, be a descent into his region. It will be a descent through the darkness of the familiar into a world where like the blind man cured in the gospels, he sees men as if they were trees, but walking.[39]

For both Caldwell and Miss O'Connor, the comic muse worked well, for it gave them the distance from which to see the world distorted and misshaped by its need to be saved.

To understand how this distancing comedy works, one may, perhaps, have to fall back on Randall Jarrell's judgment that "the best one can do with Mr. Caldwell's peculiar variety of humor is to accept it with gratitude."[40] But before one does so accept, it is well to listen to one more hard caveat from Miss O'Connor: "Even though the writer who produces grotesque fiction may not consider his characters any more freakish than ordinary fallen man usually is, his audience is going to, and it's going to ask him why he has chosen to bring such maimed souls alive. . . . in this country the general reader has managed to connect the grotesque somehow with the sentimental, for whenever he speaks of it favorably, he seems to associate it with the writer's compassion. . . .The kind of hazy compassion demanded of the writer now makes it difficult for him to be *anti* anything. Certainly when the grotesque is used in a legitimate way, the intellectual and moral judgments in it will have the ascendancy over feeling."[41]

Both Erskine Caldwell and Flannery O'Connor knew how to say "No!" in laughter.

Notes

1. "Some Aspects of the Grotesque in Southern Literature," in *The Added Dimension: The Art and Mind of Flannery O'Connor*, ed. Melvin J. Friedman and Lewis A. Lawson (New York, 1966), p. 273.

2. "The Fiction Writer and His Country" in *The Living Novel: A Symposium*, ed. Granville Hicks (New York, 1957), p. 160.

3. Review of *The Surface of Earth*, by Reynolds Price, in *New York Times Book Review*, June 29, 1975, p. 1.

4. C. Hugh Holman, *A Handbook to Literature*, 3d ed. (Indianapolis, 1972), p. 246.

5. A fine representative collection of these humorists, with a perceptive introduction is *Humor of the Old Southwest*, ed. Hennig Cohen and William B. Dillingham (Boston, 1964).

6. See C. Hugh Holman, "Simms's Changing Views of Loyalists during the Revolution," *Mississippi Quarterly*, XXIX (Fall, 1976), 501–513.

7. These novels are dealt with as comedies of manners in "April in Queenborough: Ellen Glasgow's Comedies of Manners" elsewhere in this volume.

8. See Melvin Beckman, *Faulkner: The Major Years* (Bloomington, Ind., 1966) pp. 139–59, for an excellent, succinct treatment of the structure and themes of *The Hamlet*; see also Olga W. Vickery, *The Novels of William Faulkner*, rev. ed. (Baton Rouge, La., 1964), pp. 167–208, for an examination of the themes of love (or sex) and money in the Snopes trilogy; and see also Warren Beck, *Man in Motion: Faulkner's Trilogy* (Madison, Wis., 1961) for a most detailed (but perhaps overly solemn) treatment of the trilogy.

9. For an explication of the functional role of the Lena Grove story, see C. Hugh Holman, "The Unity of Faulkner's *Light In August*," in his *The Roots of Southern Writing: Essays on the Literature of the American South* (Athens, Ga., 1972), pp. 149–67; the essay was first published in *PMLA* LXXII (Mar. 1958), 155–66.

10. *The Hamlet* (New York, 1940), pp. 28–53. This episode was originally published as a short story, "Fool About a Horse," *Scribner's*, C (Aug. 1936), 80–86.

11. *The Hamlet*, pp. 309–67. This episode was originally published as a short story, "Spotted Horses," *Scribner's*, LXXXIX (June 1931), 585–97. The story is substantially revised and greatly expanded in the novel.

12. "Caldwell: Maker of Grotesques," *The Philosophy of Literary Form: Studies in Symbolic Action*, 2d ed. (Baton Rouge, La., 1967), p. 354.

13. *Erskine Caldwell* (Minneapolis, Minn., 1969), pp. 5–8.

14. *Miss Mama Aimee* (New York, 1967), p. 79.

15. *Call It Experience* (New York, 1951), p. 101.

16. *Ibid.*, p. 132.

17. *Ibid.*, pp. 101–102.

18. "The Fiction Writer and His Country," pp. 161–62.

19. Preface to *Wise Blood*, in *Three: Wise Blood, A Good Man Is Hard to Find, The Violent Bear It Away* (New York, 1964), p. 8.

20. *The Question of Flannery O'Connor* (Baton Rouge, La., 1973), pp. 3–42.

21. "Some Aspects of the Grotesque in Southern Literature," p. 276.

22. "Good Country People," in *The Complete Stories of Flannery O'Connor* (New York, 1971), p. 291.

23. *Ibid.*, p. 272.

24. *Ibid.*, p. 273.

25, *Ibid.*, p. 276.

26. *Ibid.*, p. 288.

27. "Revelation," in *The Complete Stories*, p. 491–92.

28. New York, 1955.

29. New York, 1952.

30. These stories, now available in *The Complete Stories*, are "The Train" (*Sewanee Review*, Apr. 1948), "The Peeler" (*Partisan Review*, Dec. 1949), "The Heart of the Park," (*Partisan Review*, Feb. 1949), and "Enoch and the Gorilla" (*New World Writing*, Apr. 1952).

31. "The Geranium," *Accent* IV (Summer 1946), 245–53. It was submitted Feb. 7, 1946, forty-five days before her twenty-first birthday (see "Notes," *The Complete Stories*, p. 551).

32. In *New World Writing* XIX (1961) and reprinted posthumously in *Everything That Rises Must Converge* (New York, 1965).

33. *Esquire* LXIII (Apr. 1965), 76–78, 151–55; reprinted in *Everything That Rises*.

34. Quoted by Robert Giroux in his Introduction to *The Complete Stories*, pp. xvi–xvii.

35. "Her Rue with a Difference," in Holman, *Roots of Southern Writing*, pp. 177–86; originally published in *The Added Dimension*, pp. 73–87.

36. "The View from the Regency Hyatt," in *Roots of Southern Writing*, pp. 96–107; originally published in *Southern Fiction Today: Renascence and Beyond*, ed. George Core (Athens, Ga., 1969), pp. 16–32.

37. Nathaniel Hawthorne, "The Old Manse," *Mosses from an Old Manse* (Boston, 1883), p. 13.

38. "Caldwell: Master of Grotesques," p. 352.

39. "Some Aspects of the Grotesque in Southern Literature," p. 279.

40. As quoted by Carvel Collins, in *Erskine Caldwell's Men and Women* (Boston, 1961), p.7.

41. "Some Aspects of the Grotesque in Southern Literature," p. 275.

Anodyne for the Village Virus

In the middle western and north central states the land is vast, the weather vicious with frigid winters and flaming summers, —and until recently—the settlements have been few and small, and the people lonely. The wind can sweep across a thousand miles to roar against a small town of a thousand citizens and make them huddle together against its fury. The human spirit is put to special tests here, and the people—the children of immigrants from Scandinavia, Germany, and Central Europe as well as the dominant New Englanders whose Puritanism gives a vise-like strength to the primitive culture—feel the weight of weather, of a close community, of confining evangelical religion. There are two sentimental traditions of such small towns, as Sinclair Lewis asserted in *Main Street*: one is that "the American village remains the one sure abode of friendship, honesty, and clean sweet marriageable girls"; the other is that "the significant features of all villages are whiskers, iron dogs upon lawns, gold bricks, checkers, jars of gilded cat-tails, and shrewd comic old men who . . . ejaculate 'Waal, I swan.'" These traditions have little similarity to actual life in the small towns of this vast region.

The Middle West and the West have taken two anodynes against the waste of spirit and the harsh weight of care of which life can consist on the Great Plains. These anodynes are romantic idealization and self-mocking and sardonic laughter. The romantic idealization has elevated the lonely man, almost always on horseback, into a figure of great force, energy, and—above all—freedom. He is the plainsman, the cowboy, the Indian fighter—a man secure in himself and his skills, a creature of epic proportions. From James Fenimore Cooper's *The Prairie* to Jack Schaeffer's *Shane*, he has dominated the land like a demigod and embodied in his ideal self the aspirations of the little men huddling for comfort against the blank and threatening vastness of the land stretching between the Ohio River and the Rocky Mountains.

The other anodyne has been laughter, but it is a comedy at some variance from the exuberance and wildness and high-spirited extravagance of the Southwest. It has smacked more of New England than of Arkansas or Texas. It has more nearly echoed Seba Smith's Major Jack Downing than George Washington Harris's Sut Lovingood. It has stayed closer to actuality than southern humor has with its wild anecdotes and exuberant actions. It has been more likely to be an essay than a tall tale, an acid comment on human frailty than a hilarious record of absurdity. Of the two main streams of native American humor which Constance Rourke defined, the West has drawn its major resources from the Yankee rather than the southern stream, and has directed them against the institutions within which the laughers themselves have lived. Western comedy is social and satiric; it is, if not sober, at least serious; and it is deeply ironic in its view of the world. A major target for its attack early became the villages dotted at widely spaced intervals on the vast middle western landscape. The dreariness and quiet despair of life in these lonely towns could catch at the throat with a pathos that approached the tragic, as it did in Willa Cather's story "The Sculptor's Funeral" and in Sherwood Anderson's *Winesburg, Ohio*. It could arouse the anger of Hamlin Garland in *Main-Traveled Roads* or Joseph Kirkland in *Zury, The Meanest Man in Spring County* or E.W. Howe in *The Story of a Country Town*. But these towns could be and characteristically were handled with irony tempered with a sense of the comic. Excellent examples of such treatment, in addition to such Mark Twain pieces as "The Man That Corrupted Hadleyburg," are the *Fables in Slang* of George Ade. One of these "Fables," first published in 1900, illustrates the essayistic, "Yankee" manner and the use of the small town as humorous butt. It is "The Fable of the Slim Girl Who Tried to Keep a Date That Was Never Made," and the first half of it goes like this:

Once upon a Time there was a slim Girl with a Forehead which was Shiny and Protuberant, like a Bartlett Pear. When asked to put Something in an Autograph Album she invariably wrote the Following, in a tall, dislocated Back-Hand:

"Life is Real; Life is Earnest,
And the Grave is not its Goal."

That's the kind of Girl she was.

In her own Town she had the Name of being a Cold Proposition, but that was because the Primitive Yokels of a One-Night Stand could not Attune Themselves to the Views of one who was troubled with Ideals. Her Soul Panted for the Higher Life.

Alas, the Rube Town in which she Hung Forth was given over to Croquet, Mush and Milk Sociables, a lodge of Elks, and two married Preachers who doctored for the Tonsilitis. So What could the Poor Girl do?

In all the Country around there was not a Man who came up to her Plans and Specifications for a Husband. Neither was there any Man who had any time for Her. So she led a lonely Life, dreaming of the One—the Ideal. He was a big and pensive Literary Man, wearing a Prince Albert coat, a neat Derby Hat and godlike Whiskers. When He came he would enfold Her in his Arms and whisper Emerson's Essays to her.

But the Party failed to show up.

Could her name have been Carol Kennicott and the name of the town be Gopher Prairie?

One of the most mordant attacks on village life and the way in which it stultifies and poisons the individual came with Edgar Lee Masters' *The Spoon River Anthology* in 1915, a collection of poems supposedly spoken by the dead who lie in the Spoon River cemetery, and describing their lives of frustration, despair, constraint, and suffering. These poems in a flat, effective, and strangely powerful free verse, together comprise a picture of life in a small town. Many of them are grim and dark; all are marked by irony that, although never happy, is often bitterly comic, as in Hod Putt's speech:

Here I lie close to the grave
Of Old Bill Piersol,
Who grew rich trading with the Indians, and who
Afterwards took the bankrupt law
And emerged from it richer than ever.

Myself grown tired of toil and poverty
And beholding how Old Bill and others grew in wealth,
Robbed a traveler one night near Proctor's Grove,
Killing him unwittingly while doing so,
For the which I was tried and hanged.
That was my way of going into bankruptcy.
Now we who took the bankrupt law in our respective ways
Sleep peacefully side by side.

Masters' Spoon River is grimly comic, and its dead speak a series of dark judgments framed in formal, almost legalistic language.

Ring Lardner was a humorist, where Masters actually was not. Their views of the middle western small towns were remarkably alike, but there the similarity stopped, for Lardner was a superb master of the spoken language and he created a long line of characters whose idiom was recorded with great precision, while the frequently vain and empty man behind the words stood forth sharply revealed. Lardner had a wild, delightful, manic quality that could erupt into nonsensical laughter, as in one of his parody plays, "I Gaspiri," in which two strangers meet and this dialogue ensues:

First Stranger: Where was you born?
Second Stranger: Out of wedlock.
First Stranger: That's mighty pretty country around there.

This wild play with words mixed together in inspired illogic although they sound as though they should make sense was Lardner's particular gift, and he used it with great skill in his hundreds of parodies. He took the lines:

Night and day under the hide of me
There's an Oh, such a hungry yearning, burning inside of me,

from Cole Porter's song, "Night and Day" which he declared shows up W.S. "Gilbert himself as a seventh-rate Gertrude Stein," and ran seven insane variations on them, including:

Night and day under the bark of me
There's an Oh, such a mob of microbes making a park of me.

51

and

> Night and day under my tegument
> There's a voice telling me I'm he, the good little egg you meant.

In the early part of his career, this language gift was employed in drawing comic pictures of small town people. His first collection of stories, *You Know Me Al* (1916) is a series of letters written by a baseball player Jack Keefe to his best friend. These letters capture perfectly the half-literate middle western speech of the protagonist, who is gullible, stupid, conceited, and totally ignoble. Hilariously funny, the tales can almost sicken the reader with their picture of human depravity. Lardner followed this book with many others, among the best being *Gullible's Travels*, in which Mr. Gullible recounts in the exact language of his middle western world the tortures of a vacation trip that he and his wife make. Mr. Gullible's account is filled with the illogic of average speech, with non sequiturs, and with such perfect uses of zeugma as "After supper we said good-bye to the night clerk and twenty-two bucks." This use of a cliché-laden vernacular was his primary means of showing up, without comment, the mindlessness, cunning, and selfishness of the average American. Perhaps his supreme picture of the middle western small town is in "Haircut," a monologue by a barber Whitey, who tells the story of Jim Kendall, his cruelty to his wife and children, and his death, without ever understanding the meaning of what he is telling. It fits perfectly George Whicher's description of Lardner's specialty as being "his ability to report with seeming unconsciousness the appalling mediocrity and vanity of the middle-class soul." As Lardner's career developed, he moved further and further from the provincial life which he began by depicting with precise ironic truth, and he wrote more and more about the world of suburbanites and of life on Long Island, in New York City, and in Florida, but he never lost his skill with language, his comic sense of incongruity, or his pessimistic despair.

Sinclair Lewis, America's first Nobel laureate in literature, was the summation and epitome of the satiric and comic reaction to what he labeled as the "Village Virus." Indeed, the Nobel citation read: "The 1930 Nobel Prize in Literature is awarded to Sinclair Lewis for his powerful and vivid art of description and his ability to use wit and humor in the creation of original characters." A native of Sauk Centre, Minnesota, Lewis was educated at Oberlin College and Yale University. In the 1920s he turned his attention back to the country of his childhood and adolescence and produced five novels that, despite a number of obvious weaknesses, seem to have a secure place in our national literature. These novels are *Main Street*, a satiric portrait of a small town huddled on the Great Plains; *Babbitt*, a portrait of a representative businessman in a typical small city in the Middle West; *Arrowsmith*, a portrait of the scientist as saint, of a physician pursuing truth with unselfish and absolute commitment, and an attack on the society that tries to inhibit and pervert his search; *Elmer Gantry*, a savagely comic portrait of a dishonest and insincere minister and of the world in which he works; and *Dodsworth*, a mellower satire, this time of Americans seeking culture in Europe. He was to produce ten more novels before his death in 1951, but none of them had the energy, vitality, and originality of the five which established his fame and, in fact, said just about all that he had to say of a world that he both loved and mocked for its painful inadequacies. Yet most of the novels published after *Dodsworth* remained grounded in the life of the Middle West, were couched in the language of the earlier works, and maintained many of the same attitudes, although mellowed by time, of his earlier years.

Lewis was originally taken as a realist, partly because his great power of mimicry gave an apparent authenticity to the speech of his characters and partly because the massive research which he did in getting the surface details of the daily lives of his people precisely right cast an air of great accuracy over the world he represented. But Sinclair Lewis was really a satirist and a humorist, and in his use of the devices and methods of the satirist and humorist lie both his greatest strengths and his chief weaknesses.

As a humorist he belongs clearly in the tradition of Yankee

humor, that of the shrewd and knowing peddler or the cracker-box philosopher. For the most important person in Lewis's best work is Lewis himself. It is he who sees with great clarity, describes with deflating directness, mocks, sneers at, condemns. Everywhere in his novels—and particularly in *Main Street* and *Babbitt*—the reader is listening to the narrator-novelist and indeed is being invited to share with him his sense of the incongruity and falseness of the world being described. Thus the novels become extended comic and satiric essays, with narrative exempla to illustrate and underscore the points. The most common posture of the narrator is that of detached observer and sardonic critic. The characters are seen from the outside, their words checked against their deeds, their actions presented mockingly. When we enter their thoughts, it is seldom to explore them as fully realized characters but rather to pinpoint a motive or make ridiculous an aspiration or dream. For example, when Carol Kennicott, in *Main Street*, is putting out plants in a park near the railroad station, Lewis says: "Passengers looking from trains saw her as a village woman of fading prettiness, incorruptible virtue, and no abnormalities . . . and all the while she saw herself running garlanded through the streets of Babylon." Certainly the interior glimpse is not intended to make an exploration of psychological depths but to deflate and to mock. The original plan of *Babbitt* was that it should represent a typical day in the life of a typical businessman. That plan still survives in the first seven chapters, one-fourth of the total book, and it is only after this eventless and typical day that the casual plot of Babbitt's futile efforts at rebellion get underway. Lewis's statement about Elmer Gantry is not unusual: "He had been sitting with a Bible and an evening paper in his lap, reading one of them." Nor is the description of Gantry praying in the pulpit of his church: "He turned to include the choir, and for the first time he saw that there was a new singer, a girl with charming ankles and lively eyes, with whom he would certainly have to become well acquainted. But the thought was so swift that it did not interrupt the paean of his prayer." No, Lewis is not drawing extended psychographs of people; he is exhibiting specimens as though they were insects in a display case, and when he penetrates their skin it is primarily to make them squirm.

This narrator is superior to his subjects. In the five big novels he presents only two characters who are treated with full sympathy, Martin Arrowsmith and Sam Dodsworth, and one, Carol Kennicott of *Main Street*, whom he likes but frequently mocks. The superiority he feels toward his people is based on his greater knowledge and his distance from them but, most important of all, it is based on his moral sense. To find the standard against which to measure these people in establishing this judgment of their morality, Lewis looks toward the past. He finds it in the sturdy pioneers, whom he often celebrates. *Main Street* begins: "On a hill by the Mississippi where Chippewas camped two generations ago. . ." And it goes on to say, "The days of pioneering, of lassies in sunbonnets, and bears killed with axes in piney clearings, are deader now than Camelot; and a rebellious girl is the spirit of that bewildered empire called the American Middlewest." *Arrowsmith* opens with the protagonist's great-grandmother, as a girl of fourteen, driving a wagon in the Ohio wilderness in the face of great adversity. It is what the towns and cities, the practices of business and the conventions of so-called polite society do to these pioneer virtues that Lewis is attacking, and it is the individualism and rugged independence which the pioneers exemplify to him that he laments the passing of. It is little wonder that that most antisocial of American individualists, Henry David Thoreau, should have been one of his ideals.

This narrator is brash and even outrageous in his style. He flings at his satiric target not merely the customary satiric methods, but he brightens and sharpens his writing with vigorous metaphors. In *Elmer Gantry* he describes the workers in the "Charity Organization Society" as being "as efficient and as tender as vermin-exterminators," and he says of a saloon that "it had the delicacy of a mining camp minus its vigor." In *Main Street* he says that the people at a party "sat up with gaiety as with a corpse." He declares of Terwillinger College, "You would not be likely to mistake Terwillinger College for an Old Folks' Home, because on the campus is a large rock painted with class numerals." Sometimes he writes scenes that are clearly boisterous comedy, such as this one about Elmer Gantry: "Elmer's eloquence increased like an August pumpkin. He went into the woods to practise. Once a small boy came up behind him, standing on a stump in a clearing, and upon being greeted with 'I denounce the abominations of your lascivious and voluptuous, uh, abominations,' he fled yelping, and never again was the same care-free youth."

Lewis is a satirist above all other things. While satire is often comic, its object is not to evoke mere laughter but laughter for a corrective purpose. It always has a target, an object which it attacks, such as pretense, falsity, deception, arrogance; and this target is held up to ridicule by the satirist's unmasking it. The satirist's vision is ultimately that of the cold-eyed realist, who penetrates shams and pretenses to reveal the truth. The simplest kind of satire is invective—that is, forthright and abusive language directed against a target so that it makes a sudden revelation of a damaging truth. Another kind of direct satire is exaggeration, by which the good characteristics are reduced and the evil or ridiculous ones are increased. Indirect satire whereby characters render themselves ridiculous by their actions and their speech is more subtle. Lewis as a satirist is usually direct and blunt. His favorite devices are invective and caricature, and in his role of unabashed and self-conscious narrator he can apply these methods directly.

His invective can be devastating. He wrote of small town ladies as "creamy-skinned fair women, smeared with grease and chalk, gorgeous in the skins of beasts and the bloody feathers of slain birds, playing bridge with puffy pink-nailed jeweled fingers, women who after much expenditure of labor and bad temper still grotesquely resemble their own flatulent lapdogs." He described a group of small town citizens as a "Sunday-afternoon mob staring at monkeys in the Zoo, poking fingers and making faces and giggling at the resentment of the more dignified race." He described Gantry as being like his watch, "large, thick, shiny, with a near-gold case," and declared, "He was born to be a senator. He never said anything important, and he always said it sonorously." College teachers were, he said, "spending the rest of their lives reading fifteenth-hand opinions, taking pleasant naps, and drooling out to yawning students the anemic and wordy bookishness which they called learning." Of a Mrs. Bogart, a Good Influence, he wrote, "Mrs. Bogart was not the acid type of Good Influence. She was the soft, damp, fat, sighing, indigestive, clinging, melancholy, depressingly hopeful kind. There are in every large chicken-yard a number of old and indignant hens who resemble Mrs. Bogart, and when they are served at Sunday noon dinner, as fricasseed chicken with thick dumplings, they keep up the resemblance."

Of course, this kind of invective leads very directly to caricature, in which the bad is exaggerated and the good reduced. For example Carol in *Main Street* went calling on Mrs. Lyman Cass, and Lewis wrote that she "pounced on . . . the hook-nosed consort of the owner of the floor-mill. Mrs. Cass's parlor belonged to the crammed-Victorian school. . . . It was furnished on two principles: First, everything must resemble something else. A rocker had a back like a lyre, a near-leather seat imitating tufted cloth, and arms like Scotch Presbyterian lions; with knobs, scrolls, shields, and spear-points on unexpected portions of the chair. The second principle of the crammed-Victorian school was that every inch of the interior must be filled with useless objects." Lewis then gives a detailed and hilarious listing of the contents of the parlor. The intention and the result are caricature.

Another kind of exaggeration results from a literal-minded reductio ad absurdum, as in the assertion that "the Maker of a universe with stars a hundred thousand light-years apart was interested, furious, and very personal about it if a small boy played baseball on Sunday afternoon." Lewis is a master of this kind of literal statement for satiric ends, as in "In the spring of '18 he was one of the most courageous defenders of the Midwest against the imminent invasion of the Germans." Carol Kennicott observes, "The respectability of the Gopher Prairies . . . is reinforced by vows of poverty and chastity in the matter of knowledge. Except for a half dozen in each town the citizens are proud of that achievement of ignorance which it is so easy to come by." In examining what religious training gave Gantry, Lewis said, "Sunday School text cards! True, they were chiefly a medium of gambling, but as Elmer usually won the game (he was the first boy in Paris to own a genuine pair of loaded dice) he had plenty of them in his gallery, and they gave him a taste for gaudy robes, for marble columns and the purple-broidered palaces of kings, which was later to be of value in quickly habituating himself to the more decorative homes of vice."

One of the qualities of Lewis's work that is difficult to describe or analyze is the way in which he can take the speech of his people, weave it into a monologue or an address, and make of it a severe indictment of the speaker, and yet appear at no point to be exaggerating the normal talk of such men. For example, this monologue from *Babbitt*: "Every small American town is trying to get population and modern ideals. And darn if a lot of 'em don't put it across! Somebody starts panning a rube crossroads, telling how he was there in 1900 and it consisted of one muddy street, count 'em, one, and nine hundred human clams. Well, you go back there in 1920, and you find pavements and a swell little hotel and a first-class ladies' ready-to-wear shop—real perfection, in fact! You don't want to just look at what these small towns are, you want to look at what they're aiming to become, and they all got an ambition that in the long run is going to make 'em the finest spots on earth—they all want to be just like Zenith!" As Edgar Johnson has observed, "Burlesque there is in Lewis, but when we try to put a finger on it, in Babbitt's speech before the Real Estate Board, Luke Dawson's opinions on labor unions, or 'Old Jud's Y.M.C.A. evangelism', it is embarrassingly apt to melt away and turn into realism. Mainly it is a matter of proportion rather than detail."

Some of Lewis's satire results from extravagant exaggeration with a perfectly straight face. An example is the section on

"Weeks" in Chapter XXI of *Arrowsmith*; "If an aggressive, wide-awake, live-wire, and go-ahead church or chamber of commerce or charity desires to improve itself, which means to get more money, it calls in those few energetic spirits who run any city, and proclaims a Week. This consists of one month of committee meetings, a hundred columns of praise for the organization in the public prints, and finally a day or two on which athletic persons flatter inappreciative audiences in churches or cinema theaters, and the prettiest girls in town have the pleasure of being allowed to talk to male strangers on the street corners, apropos of giving them extremely undecorative tags in exchange for the smallest sums which those strangers think they must pay if they are to be considered gentlemen."

Lewis holds the middle western world up to Juvenalian laughter, points with unmistakable directness to its weaknesses and errors, and, as satirists have always done, seems to hope that seeing itself in the steel mirror of his description will make it repent and improve. In *Main Street* he declares of the small town:

> It is an unimaginatively standardized background, a sluggishness of speech and manners, a rigid ruling of the spirit by the desire to appear respectable. It is contentment . . . the contentment of the quiet dead, who are scornful of the living for their restless walking. It is negation canonized as the one positive virtue. It is the prohibition of happiness. It is slavery self-sought and self-defended. It is dullness made God.
>
> A savorless people, gulping tasteless food, and sitting afterward, coatless, and thoughtless, in rocking-chairs prickly with inane decorations, listening to mechanical music, saying mechanical things about the excellence of Ford automobiles, and viewing themselves as the greatest race in the world.

Here the outrage and anger are not masked, the comic cushion is not present. The point of view that leads the narrator through his long attack on the people of the books is present in red-faced anger. But such direct statement is unusual in Lewis.

Even at his solemnest moments, wit and the comic spirit usually cloak his rage. In a statement that is almost a declaration of faith for Lewis, he describes Martin Arrowsmith as preaching

to himself "the loyalty of dissent, the faith of being very doubt-
ful, the gospel of not bawling gospels, the wisdom of admitting
the probable ignorance of one's self and of everybody else, and
the energetic acceleration of a Movement for going very slow."
In that series of witty paradoxes on a most serious subject Lewis
is very much himself. If the paradox undercuts a little the seriousness of the portrait of Martin Arrowsmith, it enhances the
role that Lewis the narrator wants to play. If his form is nearer
essay than fiction, if his laughter is more embittered and angry
than exuberant or outgoing, if his view of men and institutions
is that of Juvenal and not Horace—that is merely another way
of saying that he is of the Middle West and its towns and Main
Streets, and while satiric laughter is an anodyne for what he
feels there, he wants it to be more than an analgesic, he wants it
to be a specific for the disease that causes the pain. If, as Mark
Schorer has said, "he gave us a vigorous, perhaps a unique
thrust into the imagination of ourselves," he intended the thrust
to be therapeutic. If it has not been, then we are the poorer for
its failure.

Lewis has by no means been the only one who has raised a
mocking and satiric voice against the loneliness, the drabness,
and the howling winds of the midwestern village, but, more effectively than the others—perhaps as effectively as the current
users of "Black Humor"—he found in sardonic laughter an effective anodyne for the village virus.

Marquand, Novelist of Manners

John Phillips Marquand was for almost forty years a highly re-munerated writer of short stories and serials for the mass circulation magazines. But, although much of his career was spent as a dependable producer of a kind of fiction which the protagonist of *Wickford Point* called "that half-world of the imagination governed by editorial fact," he began in 1937 pub-lishing distinguished novels of manners, in which he gave firm, skillful, accurate, and ironic representations of the upper-class and upper-middle-class social world. In 1949 he declared, "I would like, before I'm through, to have a series of novels which would give a picture of a segment of America during the past fifty years." In his nine novels of manners he succeeded to a de-gree that makes him an important—although often neglected—figure in contemporary American fiction.

When he published *The Late George Apley*, after fifteen years as a "front cover name" for the *Saturday Evening Post*, he was greeted with critical enthusiasm, treated as a redeemed penitent, and expected to cry "Mea culpa" and sin no more. Yet, while he certainly grew restive under its conventions, Mar-quand never developed a contempt for popular fiction. So he continued to write it, although at a decreased rate, to the dis-tress of some of his critics and the silence of a growing number of those who had taken him seriously in the late 1930s. The last three of his works published before his death were *Life at Happy Knoll*, a collection of amusing and lightly satiric stories about a country club, originally published in *Sports Illustrated*; *Stop-over: Tokyo*, the last (and best) of his novels of international in-trigue featuring Mr. Moto; and *Women and Thomas Harrow*, one of the best and most serious of his major novels.

Jim Calder, the writer of commercial fiction in *Wickford Point*, says, "We . . . took a pride in our product, not the wild free pride of an artist, but the solid pride of a craftsman." And, he says, "This escapist literature for a hopeless but always hopeful people possessed a quality of artisanship that demanded high technique." This artisanship Marquand could employ in the writing of popular fiction with the unabashed intention merely to entertain; and he could also use it to give his serious fiction a silky smoothness and clarity that made it attractive to a mass audience. But it rendered his serious work suspect to critics whose predilections are toward work whose difficulty is on the surface—in its use of language, of image, and of symbol —rather than in the complexities of human relationships and the ambiguities of social problems.

Marquand was not an extensive or dedicated experimenter with the art of fiction, but a practitioner of the novel of social realism as it had been developed in the nineteenth century. He tried to represent man in his social milieu and to reveal man's character through his conduct and the choices he made in his society, rather than through the exploration of the inner self. He brought to the portrayal of his middle-aged protagonists the artistic ideals of Trollope, Howells, and Henry James, and the objective of making a satiric picture of reality which he learned from Sinclair Lewis, whose work he admired greatly. Like these masters of his, he declared, "I can only write of what I know and have seen."

What he knew best when he began his career as a serious novelist was the Boston of the patrician classes, the New England of the upper middle classes, and the New York of commercial fiction and advertising. For him the most significant figure of his world seemed to be what he once called "the badgered American male—and that includes me—fighting for a little happiness and always being crushed by the problems of his environment." He was convinced that this frail and often unthinking reed was not unique to the environment in which Marquand knew him best. In 1949 in an introduction to the Modern Library edition of *The Late George Apley*, he wrote,

"The mental approach of . . . Apley . . . [is] observable in every civilization, and one which must exist whenever society assumes a stable pattern."

Yet, as he was keenly aware, America was a civilization in which society maintains no stable patterns. The American novelist who would test his characters against a static social order or fixed conventions must ultimately despair of his native land as a subject for his art, as Cooper, Hawthorne, and James had done. The impact which democracy makes on manners converts the novelist from being a tester of character by established standards to a portrayer of character under the persistent impact of change. The social novelist's subject becomes mutability rather than order, and his testing cruxes occur when change rather than stasis puts stress on the moral values of his characters. "Social mobility," a term which he borrowed from the social anthropologists, thus becomes a recurrent condition, even in Boston, in Marquand's novels. The problems of caste, class, and social movement he knew intimately, and found fascinating.

In his serious novels, Marquand drew extensive, accurate, convincing, and often uncomplimentary pictures of the world he knew best, writing of it with an ease that masked the penetration of the study which he was making. In his polished and patrician way, he defined the ambitions, the intentions, and above all the frustrations of the average moderately successful middle-aged citizen with an acuteness that made many of his readers meet his characters with a shock of self-recognition.

Although he was probably as impatient with the young existentialists as he clearly was with those who prate in Freudian terms of "free social guilt," his major novels define a moral and spiritual emptiness, a sense of loneliness and quiet despair, that is not far removed from Kafka and Sartre. The fact that his people, when they face the emptiness of their lives, take less spectacular courses than do the standard existential heroes—that they respond with a private school's "stiff upper lip" and sense of duty and dignity—should not blind us to the fact that Marquand's characters, like Hemingway's waiter, find themselves at last alone in a "clean, well-lighted place," muttering their traditional Puritan prayers to some great *nada*, whose answers are to be read in the stifling grasp of a social environment. Yet this pessimism is usually masked behind a gently ironic tone, and these characters are handled with the wry detachment of the novelist of manners and not, except in a few cases, in tragic terms or with bitterness.

Marquand's total career is remarkably like that of the protagonists of his novels, and the totality of his work, both early and late, has a unity of thrust and impact that few people have recognized—perhaps because most of those who regard the novels after *The Late George Apley* as works of art have never looked carefully at the so-called hackwork which preceded them. In fact, the shadowy outline of subject, method, and manner for the later novels is at least faintly discernible in even the earliest of Marquand's works.

John Phillips Marquand was born on November 10, 1893, in Wilmington, Delaware, where his father was working as a civil engineer for the American Bridge Company. But his New England roots stretched far back into the history of America. He was on the maternal side a direct descendant of Governors Thomas and Joseph Dudley of the Massachusetts Bay Colony, a grandnephew of Margaret Fuller, and a close relation of the Hales. The Marquands were of Norman-French descent, having migrated from the island of Guernsey to New England in 1732 and settled in Newburyport, thirty-two miles north of Boston. There they were privateers, ship builders and owners, and sea captains; for long generations before John's birth the male Marquands had been sons of Harvard, including his father Philip, who was graduated in 1889.

The early years of John's childhood were passed in some affluence. His father became a successful broker in New York City, where he bought a town house in the East 30s, was listed in the New York Social Register, and later moved to a sumptuous home with two servants and a footman at Rye. This affluence was shortlived, however, for the Panic of 1907 completely wiped out Philip Marquand's holdings. He returned to his profession, accepted an engineering job on the Panama Canal, and took his wife with him. John, then fourteen, was sent to the Marquands' ancestral home at Curzon's Mill, Kent's Island, on the Artichoke River, four miles west of Newburyport. There he lived with two aunts and a great-aunt, all maiden ladies, kins-people of the Hales and friends of John Greenleaf Whittier, who, according to rumor, often rowed across the Merrimack River from Amesbury to visit them and, perhaps, to pay quiet court to John's great-aunt, Mary Curzon. Everything in his background and tradition indicated that he would attend Groton, Exeter, St. Mark's, or some other illustrious private school, but there was nothing in the family coffers to make it possible.

Thus the impoverished inheritor of a distinguished social and intellectual tradition attended the public high school in New-buryport and experienced "downward mobility." He applied for the scholarship which the Newburyport Harvard Club gave, but his application was rejected. He then secured a schol-arship awarded by a fund established to finance at Harvard students committed to the study of scientific subjects. There he made none of the clubs, despised the chemistry which he was pledged to study, and won what modicum of fame was to be his through work on the *Lampoon*. In his sketch of himself for the twenty-fifth anniversary of his class he wrote: "Harvard is a subject which I still face with mixed emotions. I brought away from it a number of frustrations and illusions which have hand-icapped me throughout most of my life." Thus he resembled those many protagonists of his whose fathers are failures—however charming—and who suffer the snubs of a public school boy among private school graduates. And it was also lit-tle wonder that much of his early historical fiction looked back with longing nostalgia to those days of New England's past when his ancestors dominated Newburyport and stretched out through their trading ships to touch the remote corners of the great world.

But if Harvard gave him little chemistry and less comfort, it did introduce him to the delights of books and writing. Upon graduation he was hired by the *Boston Evening Transcript*, that Bible in newsprint for the Brahmin Boston of the time. He began as a reporter at fifteen dollars a week; he was transferred to the twice-weekly magazine section, and, at the end of a year, he was raised to twenty-five dollars a week. However, about this time Battery A of the Massachusetts National Guard, which he had joined while he was at Harvard, was mobilized and sent to the Mexican border. In July 1916, he became a private in a military unit made up largely of Boston's socially elite and was sent to El Paso, Texas, where he manicured the horses and kept the stables clean.

In April 1917, Marquand went to the Officers' Training Camp at Plattsburg, New York, where he worked hard and headed the first lieutenants' list when his class completed its training in August. He arrived in France as an officer of the Fourth Division, Artillery Brigade Headquarters. He fought well as a combat soldier with the 77th Regiment Field Artillery at the Vesle River, at Saint-Mihiel, and in the Argonne. He was under shellfire many times and survived two gas attacks.

He sailed from Brest on November 2, 1918, to join a new division in America as a captain, but when the ship arrived in the New York harbor the Armistice had been signed, and Marquand was demobilized. He was impressed, he later said, with the changes that had occurred. "America, when I had left it, had been an orderly place, and now it was seething with all sorts of restive discontent. . . . It all adds up now in my memory to maladjustment and discomfort, disbelief in old tradition and suspicion of the present and the future." These experiences were to form one of his major subject matters, and the painful sense of change was to remain hauntingly with him.

He got a job on the magazine section of the *New York Tribune*, but he soon moved, with Robert Benchley's aid, to the J. Walter Thompson Advertising Agency, where he worked as copywriter on advertising campaigns for Blue Buckle Overalls, O'Sullivan's Rubber Heels, and Lifebuoy soap. Although he sensed, he later said, that "There began to be a new type of hero in this postwar world . . . the business man," he himself disliked this new man's world very much.

When he had saved four hundred dollars, he resigned and went to the Marquand place at Curzon's Mill to write a novel, *The Unspeakable Gentleman*, a tale of Newburyport in the year 1805. His narrator, Henry Shelton, was a man looking back upon an experience of his youth; Shelton's father was "the unspeakable gentlemen," a charming and deadly rascal, engaged in a complex French royalist plot and accompanied by a beautiful and mysterious French lady. The plot is made up of extravagant derring-do, and its characters are given to striking preposterous poses. Yet *The Unspeakable Gentleman* bears a significant relationship to much of Marquand's later writing: it is concerned with the New England past; its narrator-protagonist is by birth a member of the ruling class who has been brought to lowly and humiliating station by the actions of his father; and it demonstrates Marquand's concern with the past viewed from the vantage point of a later time. For example, its fifth chapter begins, "Even today, as I pen these lines, the picture comes back with the same intensity, but little mellowed or softened with the years." In 1940, Marquand said, "I meant every word of it when I did the work. It was in every way the best I could do at the time—and that goes for everything I've done since."

The *Ladies' Home Journal* paid $2,000 for the novel and published it as a serial in 1921; Scribner's issued it as a book in 1922, and it sold 6,000 copies; his career as a professional writer was launched with what appeared to be spectacular success. In 1921 he had sold a short story to the *Saturday Evening Post*; now he began selling more of them and showed sufficient promise to be unsuccessfully solicited by Ray Long, the editor of *Cosmopolitan*, to become one of his "regulars."

Also in 1921, flushed with the sale of *The Unspeakable Gentleman*, he had made a trip to Europe, the first of a great many journeys to far places, which by the end of his life had taken him —for pleasure, for material for stories, or from military necessity

—to most of the familiar spots and many of the forgotten corners of the earth. In 1949 he could say, "I have seen the Assam Valley, Bushire in Persia, the Gobi Desert, the Sahara Desert, the Andes, Iceland, Ascension Island, Lake Chad, the Amazon, the Nile, the Ganges, the Coliseum and the Taj Mahal." He was several times in China—Peking he thought the most interesting city in the world—and in Japan, Manchukuo, Egypt, Arabia, Central Africa, and the Amazon Valley. Despite the fact that, as he often expressed it, "always his steps were turning home," Marquand was a restless man; he felt the call of far places, and his delight in other social and cultural patterns was strong. He was particularly impressed with the Chinese concept of *fêng-shui*, which he thought of as "the balance of things." It was the statement of a Chinese soothsayer that he needed a mustache for *fêng-shui* that led him to grow a small one which he wore for the remainder of his life.

On this first of many journeys, he became engaged in Rome to Christina Sedgwick, whom he had met a year before in New Hampshire, and to whom he was married on September 8, 1922, in Stockbridge, Massachusetts. She belonged to one of the most important New England families and was the niece of Ellery Sedgwick, who, as editor of the *Atlantic Monthly*, was the literary arbiter of Boston. This marriage brought him, he said, "face to face with the capitalist system." The couple settled in Boston in an old house on Beacon Hill; Marquand joined the Tavern and Somerset clubs, purchased a share in the Athenaeum Library, hired a maid-of-all-work, bought a car, and, upon the arrival of the first of their two children, employed a nurse. In 1949 he ruefully observed, "And ever since then I've been over a barrel."

The financial basis on which the lives of these "Proper Bostonians" rested came from Marquand's successful application of his talent and his growing technical skill in the production of fiction for the mass-circulation magazines. In the first decade of his career, between 1921 and 1931, he published five serials and fifty-nine short stories in the *Saturday Evening Post*, the *Ladies' Home Journal*, and *Collier's*. Three of the serials became books, a fourth one was combined with three short stories and published in the book *Four of a Kind* (1923). The *Post* was paying from $500 to $3,000 apiece for his short stories and from $30,000 to $40,000 each for his serials. Although he was having to write for a living, clearly the living it brought was quite good, for the Marquands were able to live in a style well known to John's ancestors but quite beyond the means of his branch of the family after 1907. But the Boston acquaintances of the Marquands had little knowledge of his literary efforts and no respect for them. His wife wanted him to try a different vein; she would have preferred that he write for her Uncle Ellery Sedgwick in the *Atlantic*—a luxury which he felt that he could not afford. "She didn't realize that my Uncle Ellery would have given me a nice silver inkwell, or a hundred dollars, and that wouldn't pay the bills," he said several decades later, when he was in a position to afford being—and, indeed, was—an *Atlantic* contributor.

In commenting on these ten years in which he learned his craft, Marquand wrote in 1954: ". . . the development of literary skills and techniques, I think, rests mainly upon personal experience. . . . Most [writers] have faced a discipline of having a list of periodicals, popular and otherwise, reject their earlier efforts. Others, in a higher income bracket, have been able to indulge in the luxury of destroying their less mature creations at the moment of production. Personally I have not been so fortunate as to have fallen into either of these categories." Hence, he learned his trade by working assiduously at it. Commercial writing demanded fine craftsmanship, even though it was expended on shallow formulas.

Most readers think of this period of Marquand's career as being given over to mystery stories and Mr. Moto's international intrigues; but these actually came later. The short stories of this period dealt with the New England past, with the Danser family and with the March family (both early forms of the Brills of Wickford Point), with prep schools and colleges, with romances of the business world and with gallant young officers in the war. O. Henry and Kipling are to be seen dimly behind them. The short novel *Only a Few of Us Left*, collected in *Four of a Kind*, is about Jimmy Lee, a sporting gentleman of the highest social order, who is to reappear with only slight modifications as Minot Roberts in *So Little Time*.

The Black Cargo (a serial published as a book in 1925) returns to the history of Newburyport. Charles Jervaile, the narrator, is looking backward to his youth. His ineffectual father had been dispossessed, and Charles was engaged in a struggle to regain the place that was rightfully his. Much of the book, loaded with a nostalgic romanticism, takes place on Yankee trading ships in the Pacific. At this time, Marquand had a strong desire to escape into the past. "I wanted to be lost in it . . . I was . . . in love with candlelight and old ships," he said.

Fourteen stories published in the *Post* in 1929 and 1930 trace the rise and slow decay of the Swales, who built and ruled Haven's End (a fictional counterpart of Newburyport), and the gradual economic growth of the lowly Scarlets, keepers of taverns and makers of shoes, who come to own Haven's End without gaining an attendant social position. Ten of these tales, ranging from the seventeenth to the twentieth century, Marquand revised and published as the book *Haven's End* (1933), which shows his growing concern with the process of social change. One result of his interest in the New England past was a biography, *Lord Timothy Dexter of Newburyport, Mass.* (1925), a record in mannered style and with arch scholarship of a notorious New England eccentric. He revised this book extensively, particularly in tone and attitude, in the posthumously published work *Timothy Dexter Revisited* (1960), in which he shifts his concern from biographical data, whimsy, and pedantic accuracy to an attempt to understand the environment that made Dexter what he was. The revised book is an illuminating personal testament to Marquand's love of Newburyport and the New England past.

Warning Hill (a serial, published as a book in 1930) deals with the very recent past in New England, told through Tommy Michael's recollections of events during his young manhood in Michael's Harbor. Tommy's father was a fascinating and charming failure. Tommy, himself of the upper middle class, reaches, from his own ambiguous social situation, both downward toward the lower-class Streets and upward toward the upper-class Jelletts who live on Warning Hill and are the social rulers of Michael's Harbor. Tommy falls in love with Marianne Jellett, only to find that, although he amuses her, she views him as "a village boy." Tommy wins success as a golfer, goes on to Harvard where he is accepted by the "right" people, becomes an army officer, and finally achieves self-definition through his own rejection of the Jelletts. Many of the situations well known to Marquand's later readers are to be found in this novel, as are attitudes that are usually associated with the post-*Apley* period. At one place in the story, Marquand observes, "He was standing in that sunny place with his whole life in the balance, though of course he did not know. Does any one ever know until it is too late?" And another character says to Tommy, ". . . we're on the fringe of things, and we're the saddest people in the world, brought up to something that we've never had, and wishing for all sorts of things." The distance in attitude, tone, and meaning is not great between Michael's Harbor and the Clyde of *Point of No Return*; and Tommy Michael faces a situation very similar to that of Willis Wayde with the Harcourts.

By 1931, Marquand says, he was being made "restless" by the popular magazine short story. "I was violently anxious to prove that this form of writing could be popular and at the same time exhibit more serious elements." He was beginning to be concerned, he wrote, "with methods of connecting past and present in order to give reality to romance." How much of this new resolve was the result of his experiences with the stories which became *Haven's End*, how much was the result of the success— at least in a technical sense—of *Warning Hill*, and how much was connected with a personal "revolt," which occurred about this time, we cannot say, and perhaps he could not either. Of the "revolt," he declared: "I was disillusioned about a great many things, a great many people—about much that I'd had full faith in. . . . I had left my wife. There was much that had happened."

That he succeeded in the early thirties in making his "formula" stories carry what he believed to be a heavier weight of significance is shown in his 1954 selection from his short works, *Thirty Years*. In it he reprints only one story written before 1930 —"Good Morning, Major" (1926), a war story which Edward J. O'Brien included in his 1939 collection of *Fifty Best American Short Stories*. On the other hand, he selected for *Thirty Years* four stories originally published in 1930, 1931, and 1932: "Rainbows," "Golden Lads," "High Tide," and "Fourth Down." A fifth story from this period, "Deep Water," was reprinted in the 1932 *O. Henry Memorial Award Prize Stories*.

During the period between 1931 and 1934, he was also seeking new subject matter, as one can see who examines the series that appeared in the *Post* dealing with a young officer in J.E.B. Stuart's Confederate cavalry. In 1934–35 he went to the Orient looking for new material. The first fruits of the search are to be seen in *Ming Yellow* (a serial, published as a book in 1935). An adventure story laid in Peking and portions of North China, *Ming Yellow* is a combination of local color and the novel of manners. Marquand was fascinated by the way in which "form permeated every phase of personal conduct and governed every situation," and by the very complex set of standards by which the Chinese lived. Despite its indifferently managed plot *Ming Yellow* points toward the serious novelist of manners which Marquand was becoming.

Before he left for his Oriental tour in late 1934, Marquand had begun to work on *The Late George Apley*, because, as he has said, "This was the first time in a hectic period of child-rearing and bills that I could afford to write something that might not be readily salable." In March 1935, when he was in Peking, China, Mrs. Christina Marquand obtained a divorce in Pittsfield, Massachusetts. In Peking in the same year, he met Adelaide Hooker and her mother, who were on a Garden Clubs of America tour. Adelaide was rich and related by marriage to the Rockefellers. After Marquand returned to the United States in 1936, they became engaged, and they were married in 1937.

In the meantime Marquand's Oriental tour began paying off. In 1935 the *Saturday Evening Post* serialized *No Hero*, a story of adventures in Japan and Shanghai when K.C. Jones, ex-naval flyer, becomes entangled with a Japanese intelligence agent named Mr. Moto. Mr. Moto was to be a popular figure, the center of intelligence activities in five additional serials which became books as *No Hero* did. It was followed the next year by *Thank You, Mr. Moto*, a tale of the intrigues which can sweep through Peking. *Think Fast, Mr. Moto* (1937), in which a young New Englander, Wilson Hitchings, finds himself in- volved with Mr. Moto in Honolulu, was the third of the famed series. A fourth Moto serial, *Mr. Moto Is So Sorry*, appeared in 1938. It is a tale of two Americans, Sylvia Dillaway and Calvin Gates, caught in international intrigue between the Japanese and the Russians in Mongolia. The fifth book in the series, *Last Laugh, Mr. Moto*, appeared in 1942.

Among Mr. Moto's major accomplishments may have been the freeing of his creator to work on a different kind of book. For the Mr. Moto serials were enormously successful and became the basis for a popular series of motion pictures in which Peter Lorre portrayed the Japanese secret agent. In Mr. Moto Mar- quand had found a fictional character that seemed to lend him- self to extensive and highly remunerative elaboration, and a plot situation that utilized his knowledge of far places—although Mr. Moto is Japanese, the actual settings of each of these spy tales is a different segment of the Orient. Marquand involves in the Moto stories a variety of American characters—the protag- onists change for each story—while Mr. Moto remains his smil- ing self, as incredible as his name, which Marquand learned was impossible as a Japanese name long after he and Peter Lorre had made it a well-established reality in what Marquand called the "half-world of the imagination." (In the final Moto story, he apologizes repeatedly for the impossibility of the name.) It is a mistake to call Mr. Moto a detective or to call Marquand a writer of detective stories or even of mysteries in the traditional sense. These books are spy thrillers of a very high order, but they lack the tight construction of the detective story.

The final Mr. Moto story, *Stopover: Tokyo* (1957), has a situation as impressively cynical as the overpraised John Le Carré novel, *The Spy Who Came in from the Cold*, and its qualities of characterization and style are superior to Le Carré's.

The Late George Apley, which had been started in 1934 and left half-finished until 1935, was completed in 1936, when portions of it appeared as self-contained episodes in the *Saturday Evening Post*, and was published as a book in 1937. The extent to which Mr. Moto financed Marquand's rebellion against the inhibitions of the commercial writer and the restrictions of the Boston environment can be seen by examining his publications in the *Post* in 1936. In February and March *Thank You, Mr. Moto* appeared and in September and October *Think Fast, Mr. Moto*; in addition five short stories were published during the year, as well as episodes from *Apley* in November and December. Never again was Marquand to publish as much in a single year. The success of *The Late George Apley*, which won the Pulitzer Prize in 1938, gave his career a new direction, a seriousness that it had not had before, and—ironically—a financial success greater than he had dreamed of in the days when he was writing commercial fiction exclusively. *Apley*, conceived, Marquand said, as "a savage attack on the old water side of Beacon Street" and presented as a parody of the "collected letters" with commentary, was the first of three satiric studies of Boston which Marquand was to write.

After the publication of *Apley* he continued, on a diminished scale, his writing of adventure serials: in 1937 he published in the *Post* the serial *3-3-8*, and in 1938, the serial version of *Mr. Moto Is So Sorry* appeared in the *Post* and *Castle Sinister* was serialized in *Collier's*. Much of *Wickford Point* was serialized in a modified form in the *Post* in early 1939; it appeared in book form as his second major novel late in that year. An adventure serial, *Don't Ask Questions*, also appeared in 1939. An English edition of this story was published in 1941, but it was not republished in America. The third of his major novels, *H.M. Pulham, Esquire*, was published in February 1941, after portions of it had been serialized in *McCall's*.

These three novels form a kind of triptych, defining in three sharply contrasting panels Marquand's view of Boston. *The Late George Apley* is a portrait of old Boston and its tradition, which had flowered in Concord in the mid-nineteenth century. In *Wickford Point* Marquand turned his satiric attention to a decaying family loosely bound to the Transcendentalists and themselves the possessors of a very minor nature poet in the family tree. *H.M. Pulham, Esquire* is a self-portrait of a contemporary Bostonian, a post-World War I businessman, whose ineffectual revolt against his class fails and who now believes himself to have a happier and better life than, as the reader knows, he actually does have. Taken together these three panels constitute a complex and varied definition of an attitude which dominates one segment of America and which probably is, as Mr. Marquand insisted, not unique to Boston but is to be found wherever society begins to allow the past to establish firm controls over the present.

These three novels completed what John P. Marquand had to say of Boston and its society. However, their success with the critics and in the marketplace and the successful presentation of two of them as motion pictures and one as a play established Marquand in the public view as the novelist of Boston. He was in the ironic position of having moved from the production of "popular magazine fiction" to the writing of distinguished novels only to find himself still stereotyped in his readers' minds: now as a producer of New England satiric regionalism. He was intensely aware of this tagging; he said, "Self-consciously and often with hopeful determination I have moved my characters to Hollywood, Washington, New York, and Paris, and also to New York suburbs and Palm Beach." Perhaps he moved them when the moves were not demanded or wise, but, in any case, he was not again to be primarily the portrayer of the New England Brahmin and his sterile code.

During the early forties Marquand's own experience was undergoing sufficient change to justify his shifting locales and professions in his portrayal of the segments of American society which he knew with any intimacy. In 1941 and 1942 he was in Hollywood working on dialogue for the motion picture version of *H.M. Pulham, Esquire*; these experiences formed the basis for his picture of the vulgarly opulent movie world in *So Little Time* (1943). His reaction to the Japanese attack on Pearl Harbor was strong, and the accelerating rate of change in his world, now faced with a second international war, was frightening to him. An obvious temporary casualty was his Japanese secret agent, whose penultimate appearance in *Last Laugh, Mr. Moto* showed him active in causes less our own than his earlier adventures had been. Marquand, in 1942 in a *Collier's* serial, *It's Loaded, Mr. Bauer* (published as a book in England but not in America), shifted to wartime espionage adventures in South America, but the change in locale proved unfortunate. He obviously felt an emotional affinity to the fixed social and cultural traditions of the Orient and had little sympathy for South American culture.

In 1944 Marquand became a special consultant to the secretary of war. He spent much of 1944 and 1945 in Washington in this role, and these experiences underlie the Washington sequences of *B.F.'s Daughter* (1946). In 1945 he became a war correspondent, attached to the Navy in the Pacific. The result of this effort was a series of articles in major magazines, some excellent short stories about Navy brass, and a short novel *Repent in Haste* (1945), which, although serialized in so prestigious a magazine as *Harper's*, is a very minor work, little better than the short novels he wrote in the 1920s and 1930s, despite its serious effort to portray a new generation at war. In 1944 Marquand became a member of the editorial board of the Book-of-the-Month Club, a $20,000 a year position which he thoroughly enjoyed and which he held until his death. In 1943 and 1944 he collaborated with George S. Kaufman on a dramatic version of *The Late George Apley*, which was produced with great success in 1946.

Neither of Marquand's two novels dealing with wartime

America, *So Little Time* and *B.F.'s Daughter*, is completely successful, perhaps because Marquand was writing of experiences too recent for him to have achieved the necessary detachment and perhaps, also, because he was attempting some very limited experiments with new fictional techniques. But both books are serious attempts to deal with the frighteningly fast changes that war makes. In the New England satires, the enemy appeared to be a caste-conscious society failing to respond to change. In *So Little Time* and *B.F.'s Daughter* not society but time itself is the great villain, social change is time's inevitable manifestation, and war is an accelerating device which destroys too rapidly the structure and tradition of society.

In 1949 Marquand published *Point of No Return*, usually considered to be, along with *Apley*, one of his two best works. It is the story of Charles Gray, a native of Clyde, Massachusetts, where he had been a "Spruce Street boy" in a world in which the "Johnson Street people" were the social rulers. He goes to the public high school rather than a private school and attends Dartmouth College instead of Harvard, and these stigmas of inferiority haunt him throughout his life. At the time of the forward action of the story, he is one of two middle-aged men being considered for promotion to a vacant vice-presidency in the conservative Stuyvesant Bank (apparently modeled after the Fifth Avenue Bank of New York City). He is sent on a mission to his native town, which seems to be modeled directly on Newburyport. There, in the flood of memories, he relives his childhood and youth, when his father had been a charming ne'er-do-well and Charles had almost, but not quite, married Jessica Lovell, of the upper upper class, although he was himself plainly only lower upper class. The broad outlines of Charles Gray's situation and character Marquand had experienced himself and had been sketching in his fiction for a long time; Gray is, *mutatis mutandis*, the hero of *The Unspeakable Gentleman* and of *The Black Cargo* and a close relative of Tommy Michael of *Warning Hill*.

This novel is unique in the thoroughness with which Marquand functions as a sociological analyst. For his interest is now

77

centered not so much in Charles's personal dilemma as in the world that has made him, in the pattern of social gradation and of change in Newburyport and in New York. In his analysis of the social forces of Clyde, Massachusetts, Marquand produces a significant commentary on one segment of American society. "Marquand's insights into the nuances of the social hierarchy of Newburyport, in *Point of No Return*, form," Max Lerner asserts in *America as a Civilization*, "a necessary supplement to the picture that [W. Lloyd] Warner gives of the structure of the same town." (Marquand was familiar with the work of social-anthropologist Warner which resulted in a massive, five-volume study of Newburyport. A one-volume abridgment, *Yankee City*, is now available, and it makes an illuminating commentary on Marquand's method in *Point of No Return*.)

The popularity of *Point of No Return* was immense, and, although the literary critics gave it relatively short shrift, the reviewers and social historians saw it as a major social document. Probably no other American novelist since Sinclair Lewis has examined the class structure of a small American city with the accuracy and illuminating insight that Marquand employed in this novel.

After *Point of No Return*, he was to produce three major novels. Although his earlier work clearly adumbrates these books, each of them represented a significant variation from its predecessors. Each was a study of success—its costs, its joys, and its deprivations—whereas the earlier novels had been essentially portraits of defeat. And each of the last three novels varied significantly from its predecessor in technique.

Melville Goodwin, USA (1951) is an ironic picture of the professional soldier and of the quality of the "opinion molders" who make him a kind of demigod. The professional soldier, his courage, and his code were persistent themes throughout Marquand's whole career. He once said, "I have seen more generals in my lifetime than I may have wished, and they always have fascinated me as social specimens." The novel is told by Sidney Skelton, a nationally famous radio commentator, who represents unconsciously much that is sentimentally mindless in contemporary American life. The two—Skelton and Goodwin —test each other in a richly complex satire. Misunderstood by most of the critics, who saw the book as an affirmation, *Melville Goodwin, USA* has the most skillfully ironic use of an unreliable narrator that Marquand ever attempted.

In 1950 and 1952 Marquand published the only two short stories he was truly proud of—"Sun, Sea, and Sand" and "King of the Sea." Both are satiric pictures of the idle rich in the Mulligatawny Club in the Bahamas. They were, he said, "the end result of many rather groping experiments in short fiction." He felt that he had "solved the problem of writing a story that the readers of a popular magazine might enjoy and yet a story that a few critics might take seriously." They were greeted with what Marquand in typical humorous overstatement called "restrained enthusiasm."

In 1953 Marquand suffered a heart attack, which may have led to the 1954 volume *Thirty Years*, a collection of short stories, sketches, articles, and addresses drawn from his total career and introduced by illuminating headnotes. It is to this volume and to his several recorded interviews that the critic must turn for Marquand's theory of fiction, as well as for easily accessible examples of his short stories—a form which he highly respected and in which he believed few Americans had succeeded. (He considered Hemingway the finest of American practitioners of the genre.)

In a thoughtful discussion of the novel in *Thirty Years*, Marquand embraces the realistic tradition. "A novel," he says, "is great and good in direct proportion to the illusion it gives of life and a sense of living. It is great in direct proportion to the degree it enfolds the reader and permits him to walk in imagination with the people of an artificial but very real world, sharing their joys and sorrows, understanding their perplexities." When he lists his choices for true greatness they are Balzac, Tolstoi, Dostoevski, Fielding, and Smollett.

If *Thirty Years* was a heart patient's backward glance o'er travel'd roads, its author still had much to write, both in the popular vein, where something of the Mulligatawny Club was to be present in the gentler comedy of *Life at Happy Knoll* (1957) and where Mr. Moto was to have his finest adventure in *Stopover: Tokyo* (1957), and in serious fiction.

In 1955 he published *Sincerely, Willis Wayde*, a devastating picture of the big business promoter and the Marquand book that is most nearly in the mode of Sinclair Lewis. In *Willis Wayde* Marquand for the only time in a serious novel avoids extensive use of the flashback, and centers his attention directly on his satiric butt, Willis Wayde. The result is a harsh and unsympathetic picture of a lower-middle-class boy who succeeds, through unremitting effort, in becoming what his father calls "a son of a bitch." This most pitiless of Marquand's books echoes situations which he had earlier treated with sympathy. For Wayde alone of his protagonists Marquand has contempt.

In 1958, he divorced Adelaide Hooker Marquand, and it was in a spirit of bitter reaction against women that he wrote his last novel, *Women and Thomas Harrow* (1958). (In an interview in 1959 he said, "It is a reflection on the American male of the twentieth century that only his secretary is good to him. Not his wife. The American wife in the upper brackets is aggressive, arrogant, domineering . . . She is invariably difficult.") This story about the three unsuccessful marriages of a very talented and successful playwright is a kind of ironic *The Tempest* to his career. Upon its publication he declared it to be his last novel, and the book has a twilight sense of putting away the players and closing the box in the mood of an embittered Prospero. When Tom Harrow looks back over the skillful and successful use he has made of his great dramatic powers, it is with a sense of nothingness that makes the book finally very dark indeed.

During the last decade of his life, Marquand was enjoying the fruits of success. If his stock was low with his critics, it was high with his large body of readers who poured over $10,000,000 into his bank account (much of it going for taxes, of course). He was living and working in his restored family home on Kent's Island, had an apartment in the most fashionable part of New York City, spent a lot of time in Bermuda and the Bahamas, and enjoyed the golf courses of Pinehurst, North Carolina. But if his "successful" heroes are to be taken as in any sense a reflection of their maker's feelings, Marquand's own version of the Horatio Alger story, like that of several of his heroes, found him "risen from the ranks" only to discover in the upper echelons a discontent and an emptiness that had made the game hardly worth the candle. Still, even if this attitude was, as he believed, typical of the beleaguered American male, his own experience of it was transmuted and rendered of value through the success with which he converted it into both accurate social pictures and disturbing studies of spiritual dryness.

It is hard not to hope—and, indeed, not to believe—that he was aware of this by no means small achievement before he died peacefully in his sleep in his home on Kent's Island on July 16, 1960.

Thomas Harrow had what Marquand called "the ambivalent curse of being able to be a part of things, and yet to stand away from them untouched." This quality of "double vision" Marquand himself possessed to a remarkable degree. As even a brief sketch of his life shows, his protagonists not only move about in a social world which Marquand knew intimately; they also have fundamental relationships to that world which parallel their creator's. This "ambivalent curse" enabled Marquand to employ his dry wit and astringent irony on his world and on many of his own experiences, both understanding and being amused by himself, his society, and his regular acquaintances. He once told an interviewer, "I am always critical of myself. . . . Unfortunately, by nature and by—if it may be called so— by artistic temperament, I am not bitter. If I use satire, I try to use it kindly."

In dealing with experience, Marquand was anxious to record what he called "the extraordinary panorama of society, the changes in life since the horse and wagon days." Yet in portraying that panorama, he turned, as many writers of the social novel have, to the novel of character. In *Timothy Dexter Revisited*, written at the very close of his career, he said: "I have learned something I should have learned long ago—that few

81

individuals are important in themselves. The environment that produced and tolerated Dexter is far more interesting than the man." But it is the man, revealed through the impact of that environment upon him, that is the central interest of Marquand's serious novels.

One of the obvious clues to the centrality of character in his work is the looseness and, it sometimes seems, the nonexistence of plot. Even his early adventure stories and his Mr. Moto tales have relaxed construction, and his major novels so far concentrate on character rather than event that they may seem to the casual reader to be formless, flowing with the narrator's whim. An excellent example of this quality can be shown by comparing the dramatic version of *The Late George Apley*, on which George S. Kaufman collaborated with Marquand, with the novel itself. In the stage version a unified—and virtually new— plot had to be supplied in order to give dramatic statement to the attitude of the Brahmin that was the intention of the novel.

Leo Gurko has called the similarity of Marquand's basic situations and central characters a "high-level formula." In one sense he is correct. Marquand in 1959 told an interviewer from *Cosmopolitan*, "what interests me personally in fiction is to take my central character, not in his youth or early manhood, but when he is nearly through, when he is faced with an important decision in his life. I then prefer to have him go back to his early past." The result is that seven of his nine novels of manners deal not with plots in any conventional sense but with crucial situations—what Marquand calls taking "a man facing the crisis of his life" and "show[ing] how he got there"—with the protagonist looking backward in memory to his formative years. The exceptions to this backward movement as the controlling structural pattern are in *The Late George Apley*, where an "official" biographer is writing about a deceased friend, and *Sincerely, Willis Wayde*, where the sequence of events is presented in a straightforward fashion, from childhood onward. In *Willis Wayde*, despite this chronological sequence of events, the actions are viewed from an undefined vantage point in the present. This vantage point that establishes a relationship between past and present for the chief actions through their presentation by backward looks was a hallmark of Marquand's fiction from *The Unspeakable Gentleman* onward. It is very effective in pointing up the contrast between past and present, whether it is used to create the romantic nostalgia of his historical fiction, best seen in *Haven's End*, or to explore the methods by which the actions and the environments of the past make and control the present. In *Timothy Dexter Revisited*, which emphasized the magnitude of the social changes that occurred in Marquand's lifetime, he says, "There is no use weeping over things that are gone. They can never be retrieved in their ancient combinations." These nine novels attempt not to re-create that past but to picture that part of it which survives in the memories and impression of the present.

Marquand in these books is writing of people and professions that he knew; his protagonists come from a world in which Marquand had lived; and they face—with inadequate spiritual defenses but with the self-conscious will to play their roles in a manner that gives attention to how things are done and shows a reasonable sense of decorum—problems of character and conscience that he believed to be common to his world. These similarities of structure, class, and theme have blinded those who have casually examined Marquand's work to the substantial technical achievements which in different ways mark his several books. His irritation that, as he says, "I am called by most critics meaningless and repetitious," is justified, for despite common elements that run through much of his work, neither charge can be substantiated in the fullest sense, if his work is viewed as the representation of a society and its various types through a variety of technical devices and fundamental methods.

The basic method of *The Late George Apley* is that of parody, an aping of the diction and attitudes of editors of what Marquand called the "collected letters of V.I.P.'s in Boston (and elsewhere) throughout which were scattered numerous biographical interpolations prepared by an often unduly sympathetic editor." Horatio Willing, vain, pedantic, and smug Boston "man of letters," is editing the correspondence of George

Apley, a very proper Boston Brahmin. What he is doing differs from other "official" records of its sort only in the fact that Apley's son John has insisted on the inclusion of matter usually excised. Willing's attempts to explain these events in Apley's life and certain of Apley's attitudes join with his own pedantry and pompous diction and his long, imprecise sentences to make Willing himself the chief target of Marquand's satire, and thus to create for him a role as a satiric overstatement of his society, a comic caricature—a role that is present in each of Marquand's novels. Style, it has been said, is the man; but in *The Late George Apley* it becomes a device for social criticism. The use of Willing to tell the story of Apley results in a double view of the Brahmin type and in a double portraiture that gives depth to the study; Willing is an object of satiric caricature and Apley is a more likable person caught in the same inexorable social traps as Willing is.

A comparison with Sinclair Lewis's *Babbitt* may be helpful. Both Babbitt and Apley are the products of their social worlds, however different the worlds themselves may be. Both attempt revolt and from time to time challenge their worlds. Both are fundamentally good men, and both are made into something that neither wants to be by quiet and almost continuous but invisible pressure. The authors of both books were men with unusually keen ears for the jargon of trades, professions, and social classes. It is even true—although perhaps not important —that both Lewis and Marquand were successful popular writers before they turned their hands to unkindly picturing of their contemporaries. But these similarities serve also to illuminate a fundamental difference. In *Babbitt* the voice we hear is that of Sinclair Lewis, and it is often raised in strident and unmistakable condemnation. In *Apley* Marquand never speaks, and the voice we hear is that of the narrator Willing. Lewis is not in any way a butt of his own invective, where Willing is at the center of Marquand's target. Hence we watch Babbitt from afar and feel that he is remarkably like our neighbors. But we can watch Apley more appreciatively than we can watch his narrator, and thus we can see him as in some ways like ourselves.

Marquand on one occasion spoke of this addition of parody to the epistolary form as "possibly a new addition," but it probably owes some substantial debt to W. Somerset Maugham's *Cakes and Ale*, and certainly a part of its basic impulse derives from George Santayana's *The Last Puritan*, which he called "A Memoir in the Form of a Novel," whereas Marquand subtitled *Apley* "A Novel in the Form of a Memoir."

Although the time sequences had been handled loosely in *Apley*, Marquand's next novel, *Wickford Point*, represented an apparently even looser use of time, but one which, on closer examination, is very artful. The story is presented through the reminiscences of Jim Calder, a writer of popular magazine fiction, as a series of events in the brief forward motion of the story trigger his recollections of the past, within which most of the significant action is to be found. Once more, the narrator is a lesser character than some of the people in the narrative, but Jim Calder is a more admirable person than Willing, and, indeed, has frequently been viewed as at least a semiautobiographical portrait. Edward Weeks, Sedgwick's successor as editor of the *Atlantic* and the publisher of some of Marquand's later short pieces, felt that Marquand's personal voice and views were more clearly discernible in *Wickford Point* than in any other of his novels. And certainly Jim Calder is used to say some quite uncomplimentary things about the world of commercial fiction. But Calder lacks the courage and the will to break away from a commercial writer's role and to attempt in his own right to create a truer picture of the world he knows. That important role he allows to fall to the pretentious and ludicrous middle-westerner, Allen Southby, who visits Wickford Point in order to learn enough about it to enable him to write a "serious" novel about New England life. If Calder is in part an autobiographical figure, it is as the reflector of an attitude which Marquand had experienced in the days of his popular adventure-story writing. And at the center of the story is Bella Brill, who is, as Calder suggests, a Thackerayesque woman, reminiscent of Becky Sharp or Beatrix Esmond. Jim, who has always been her confidant and to a certain extent her captive;

Joe Stowe, her former husband, whom she desires to remarry because he is a success; Howard Berg, whom she plots to marry for his money—all function to reveal her in her shallowness, selfishness, and genteel depravity. The result is a detailed, convincing, very urbane and polite study of frivolous bitchery.

Jim's diction and sentence structure are those of the professional writer, and, although ostensibly relaxed, they have a directness, a clarity, and an accuracy that Willing's had lacked. Willing writes such crabbedly pedantic sentences as this one which is a part of a description of a wedding: "It is the writer's belief that nearly any man must look back to this important period in his life with somewhat mingled emotions, in that the new social contacts and this new and beautiful relationship cannot but cause a certain amount of mental confusion." In contrast, Jim Calder writes of Bella Brill: "Bella's violet eyes were half-closed, but her lips were just a trifle grim. Her expression made me wonder if she had ever loved at all. She had certainly talked enough about it. I wondered if she had been secretly in love with her father, her brothers or her mother. Certainly she had never given any visible sign of such undeveloped weakness." Each book is, in a sense, a stylistic tour de force. But the publication of *H.M. Pulham, Esquire* revealed what many had not fully understood—that Marquand had a finely discriminating ear for American speech, a sensitivity to the significance of word choice and sentence structure that probably has not been surpassed in American writing since Mark Twain. Willing's narrative might have been a parody of a literary form, requiring sensitivity to the printed page; Calder's might have been Marquand's own voice. But Pulham's first-person narrative is a triumph of stylistic exactness. The language and attitudes of a Boston investment counsel are perfectly caught and are used successfully to portray Harry Pulham, as he reveals himself through contemplation about the writing of his "class life" for the twenty-fifth reunion of his Harvard class.

This ability to capture the very accent of American upper-middle-class and upper-class speech, to employ its jargon with authenticity, and to know the precise degree of exaggeration to use in order to point out its absurdity and pretension, Marquand was to use with increasing effectiveness. In *So Little Time*, he moves to the world of the theater, with Jeffrey Wilson, successful play-doctor who dreams of writing his own great play, while the clocks, accelerated by the outbreak of war, rush inexorably on. Marquand uses Jeff Wilson as a viewpoint character, writing of him in the third person, but employing Wilson's thoughts formulated in Wilson's style as his medium. A comparison of the style of these four books should silence all critics who accuse Marquand of self-imitation except those who are tone-deaf.

In *B.F.'s Daughter* Marquand attempts to use two viewpoint characters: Polly Fulton Brett is the principal one and Bob Tasmin is the secondary one. While he does an excellent job of creating a significantly different voice for each, the novel does not quite come off, chiefly because Polly's tone of voice seems slightly out of key. In *Point of No Return* he uses once more the viewpoint pattern of *So Little Time*, employing a third-person presentation of Charles Gray's reminiscences couched in the language of a middle-aged conservative New York banker.

In certain respects *Melville Goodwin, USA* is Marquand's greatest triumph of style. It is told in the first person by Sidney Skelton, a fairly typical mass-communications and "entertainment world" figure. But much that Skelton relays comes to him from the reminiscences of General Goodwin, as he is being interviewed by a writer from a magazine that is doing a "cover story" on him, and from conversations with the general's wife. Skelton plays a role rather like that of Horatio Willing in *The Late George Apley*, in that his language and his attitudes define him as shallow, confused, and lacking in fundamental integrity. That he develops a great admiration for General Goodwin and expresses it with vigor and at length was taken by many critics as indicative of Marquand's appreciation of the military, whereas it is in fact a satiric attack on mass-communication journalism that makes a demigod of a man of the limited mind of Melville Goodwin. The very complex criticism of value systems both in the military and in the world of "opinion molders" being made has escaped the attention of many of his readers with the result that the novel which is, in a technical sense at least, his most complex and skillful has lacked an appreciative audience. Certainly Marquand never carried his concern with point of view and style to greater lengths or employed it more effectively. Many readers who should have known better read *Goodwin* the same way that they would have read *Apley* if they had taken Willing as an admired spokesman for the author.

Sincerely, Willis Wayde by contrast is Marquand's simplest book in terms of point of view. It is a third-person narrative focused sharply on Wayde and moving forward in chronological sequence. A similar simplicity appears in *Women and Thomas Harrow*, where the third-person viewpoint reports the thoughts of Tom Harrow, but where the structure is that of the brief crucial forward movement of plot, within which the narrator recalls the pertinent parts of the past. Tom Harrow was probably speaking for his creator when he said: "I want to hear the talk . . . There are different kinds of talk. . . . I want to get it classified. . . . Some people say one thing; others with the same thoughts express them differently. Stockbrokers talk alike and bankers in a slightly different way. I like to listen for the difference."

There is basically little that is new in Marquand's fictional methods. They are those of the realist, employing an unreliable narrator who tells the story through retrospection and in the language and attitudes of the profession, class, and locale from which he comes. But the skill with which Marquand employed this method is quite unusual, and the subtlety with which he uses it for satiric portraits should never be underestimated. Command of the tools of the trade does not make a novelist great —that is a function of many factors, including the things upon which the tools are used—but such command does make a novelist a fine craftsman, and that Marquand certainly was. His clarity, sureness of touch, firmness of structure, and wit are all of a high order.

Since he centered his attention in these books on character

shaped by environment and on the tension between self and society which defines the value systems of people and the context of social structures, the test of Marquand's ultimate importance in the American novel must rest with the people he created and the problems he gave them. No other American novelist since Sinclair Lewis has had a sense of the significant social detail that is as great as Marquand's. John O'Hara sees more than Marquand but has difficulty selecting. Louis Auchincloss is certainly approaching a comparable mastery of the world of high society in New York, but so far his considerable talents and his perceptive eye have been tied to areas much narrower than Marquand's finally proved to be.

Marquand's major theme is the defeat of the self by society, and he intends this theme to have a broader basis than might appear if we think of it as the defeat of the self by a special society at a special time. One of the illuminating things about his Boston trilogy is that he covers a very broad span of years. The powerful thing that is Boston society slowly embraces the young whenever you find them, and its iron claw may express itself in various ways at different times but never painlessly.

When we look beyond the remarkable virtuosity of Marquand's narrative point of view to the central characters whose portraits he draws, we find him less a satirist than we had expected. The world he describes with all its foibles and fools is one in which he is finally comfortable if not contented. His protagonists are pleasant to meet, with few exceptions admirable to do business with, and delightful golfing companions. If they are surrounded in large measure by fools and pour out their efforts fruitlessly on unfertile soil, their lot seems to him little different from that of most "American males." If they seek but never find "the ideal woman" they partake, he feels, of the common experiences of our world.

The crucial event in most of these novels occurs at a point where the opportunity for personal choice has already passed. It does not change the character's position in the world, but rather confirms it. Titles like *So Little Time* and *Point of No Return* underscore this position. The standard Marquand hero in the past once faced the forks in Frost's yellow wood and took the road most traveled by. At that moment of choice each of them had tried to rebel without success. And now in his backward searchings each is seeking to understand the point in time when his choice of roads became irrevocable.

George Apley's rebellion centered around Mary Monahan, an Irish girl whom he loved. The family applied the standard therapy of a trip abroad and it worked in the standard way. Her reappearance to rescue him from public humiliation long after he has accepted the pattern of his world and is imposing it on his son is melodrama, finally unworthy of the seriousness of the author of the book. Jim Calder's rebellion is against the claims— emotional and familial—of Wickford Point and he would like to rebel also against the shallow commercial fiction which he writes but he recognizes, he says, that "a serious novel is a very great gamble for one who must live by writing." It is a gamble that he lacks the courage and will to make. Freedom from Wickford Point is to be found with the New York girl Pat Leighton, but only the most superficial reader will feel that his marriage to her, which constitutes the novel's apparently happy ending, can bring him the happiness which a larger rebellion—against the world of popular fiction—would have brought.

Harry Pulham, following the war, cuts the family cord for a time and tries his fortunes in New York where he works for an advertising agency and falls in love with Marvin Myles, but he returns home at last to become an investment counsel, marry the family approved Kay Motford, and settle down to a life without ecstasy or delight but with reasonable contentment. Jeffrey Wilson rebels against his wife, the way he earns his living as a play-doctor, and the exigencies of time. But his affair with Marianna Miller, an actress, and his attempt to write a great play both fail, and he settles down with admirable, stoic courage to the mixture as before. Charles Gray marries the right girl, makes the right steps, and finally sees that the vice-presidency of the bank, for which he had been struggling, is an undesirable trap but one which he cannot avoid, since he has passed "the point of no return." Both Sidney Skelton and General Melville Goodwin are discontented with their worlds, and the general tries to have an affair with Dottie Peale and leave his wife, but the military service habits are too strong and he goes back to his wife and his troops, while Skelton rises even higher in his morally precarious world.

In *Sincerely, Willis Wayde* Marquand produced his least typical book. Willis Wayde is a lower-middle-class boy befriended by the Harcourts, an old New England family of mill owners. But Willis belongs to a new, amoral, and totally selfish business world, one in which the "management team" and the organization man are at home and in control. The ethical problems which the Harcourts had taken seriously are in no sense issues for Willis or his world. Willis is, as Marquand once remarked, "quite a stinker," and in telling his story Marquand writes in bitterness and anger. In this novel, he revives situations from *Warning Hill* and *Haven's End*, but he uses them with a deepening and darkening anger. In *B.F.'s Daughter* he had portrayed Burton Fulton, a self-made businessman as he was seen by his daughter, Bob Tasmin, an aristocrat who liked him and loved Polly, and Tom Brett, the liberal New Deal bureaucrat whom Polly married. But B.F. had been a belated "robber baron," a man of great ability, great independence, and great integrity. Critics comparing B.F. and Willis Wayde have often accused Marquand of changing his mind about business, when, in fact, he is portraying two different generations. To contrast Burton Fulton and Willis Wayde is to see a shocking decay of integrity in the business world.

Shortly after the publication of *Women and Thomas Harrow*, two years before his death, Marquand said, "I have decided that I am out of the tempo of the times. Unless I go mad, I'm not going to write another novel. . . . I think when any novelist reaches the point in his career where he is out of the argot of his times, then he should stop." In this novel about a fabulously successful writer, he says much about literary success, much about writing to fit the moment's need and to make money. Thomas Harrow finds himself at last convinced that "the only true reality in the world existed there [in books]—the reality of appeal of mind to mind." When he moves from this world of the imagination to that of his daily life, he sees himself and his wife "clasped together by a hideous loneliness."

In this valedictory to the novel by Marquand, Thomas Harrow is a strangely moving figure, a man of fundamental integrity, now a little out of touch with his times and desiring to do the "right thing." He attempts suicide by wrecking his car on a guard rail at a cliff that overlooks the sea. Having failed, he figuratively picks up his burden again and drives on home to accept once more the pattern of his responsibility, however joyless. He concludes in the last sentence of the novel, "In the end, no matter how many were in the car, you always drove alone."

Within these nine novels Marquand had portrayed what he once said "interested [him] most in the phenomena of human nature—the individual caught in a pattern of social change, usually tragically." This individual he examined as Boston Brahmin, as popular writer, as Boston investment counsel, as play-doctor, as "robber baron," as conservative banker, as professional soldier, as "organization man," and as successful playwright. These men in Boston, New York, Hollywood, and Washington were caught in a rapidly changing world, marked by two great wars and a social and moral transformation. The sureties were gone, whether we judge them to be social orders, moral commitments, or religious sanctions. Tom Harrow stops by the old First Congregational Church to be greeted by the Reverend Mr. Godfrey, who preaches sermons on "How Happy Are You Inside?" and who assures Harrow that they're "both in show business." Harrow is offended and recalls the pastor who had married him and his first wife in that church, but seems not to see that the outcome of that marriage actually underscores the death of the religion under whose authority it was performed.

But if Marquand's protagonists ultimately find themselves strangers and afraid in a world of vast change, they still lack tragic proportions, because they are too easily betrayed. For example, at the end of *H.M. Pulham, Esquire*, Harry writes a conclusion to his class "life" in which he portrays himself as happy and successful—a conclusion which is seriously undercut by our knowledge that he is a cuckold. His assertion at the end of the novel also seems to mark how much he really misunderstands his world: "I cannot share with my classmates the discouragement and pessimism which has been engendered by the New Deal. It seems to me only a phase and that matters will be better soon in business and in national life. I do not believe that either Mr. Roosevelt or Germany can hold out much longer and I confidently look forward to seeing a sensible Republican in the White House." The time of that remark was 1940.

Edith Wharton once said that a "frivolous society can acquire dramatic significance only through what its frivolity destroys." Marquand seems to be saying that a staid and backward looking society can best be portrayed by what it stifles in able, good, but weak men. Thus these various protagonists become finally, not tragic figures, but standards for measuring their society. This is comedy rather than tragedy because the men and their goals lack tragic magnitude, because, deserving what they get, it becomes satirically appropriate that they should get it—and that their own recognition scenes should be wry rather than wrathful.

A great deal of the delight in reading Marquand comes from the many satiric pictures of the minor characters. The tweedy Harvard professor Allen Southby, in *Wickford Point*; the perennial old grad Bo-jo Brown, in *H.M. Pulham, Esquire*; the bureaucrat Tom Brett in *B.F.'s Daughter*; Walter Newcombe, the ignorant and pompous foreign correspondent of *So Little Time*. The list could be multiplied many times. In these minor characters a world is created with great success, its very tone and quality caught in the amber of precise language. In portraits of these people Marquand's comic powers are shown and his novels become witty representations of ourselves, viewed in the steel glass of the satirist.

Furthermore, Marquand is a social historian of considerable magnitude. He has caught the language, the cadence, the attitudes, and the absurdities of upper-middle-class America. In *So Little Time*, for example, is a remarkably accurate and complete picture of a state of mind common in America in the early forties, yet the novel is so tied to the immediate emotional pressures of its time and to precise historical events that it is his most dated book. The new breed of businessmen and the new business world are imprisoned in *Sincerely, Willis Wayde*; the temper of decayed intellectualism and excessive pride in the New England remnants of transcendentalism is defined in *Wickford Point*. Country life for the very wealthy has seldom been portrayed in its ridiculous aspects more thoroughly than through Fred and Beckie, in *So Little Time*, where life is very, very rural, and very, very simple, and the hay in the barn (used as a playroom) has been fireproofed. One of the most truly memorable of Marquand's satiric sketches is that of the social-anthropologist Malcolm Bryant, who is using techniques learned from the study of primitive cultures to examine the social structure, caste, and class distinctions (upper-upper, middle-upper, lower-upper, upper-middle, middle-middle, lower-middle, upper-lower, middle-lower, lower-lower) of Clyde in *Point of No Return*. And among the best realized of these small and totally convincing portraits done in acid is that of Walter Price, in *Women and Thomas Harrow*, who keeps endlessly constructing noble pasts for himself and who is not above declaring that he helped Shaw with *Major Barbara* and referring to F. Scott Fitzgerald as "Fitzy." Actually it is difficult to think of a foible of Marquand's world which he has not shown.

He might have been writing of himself when he said in *Women and Thomas Harrow*, "His interest in people and places never lagged, and his instinct for caricature was as good as his memory for names and places," and added, "It was his persistent curiosity that had given his work vitality." These interests united to a remarkably accurate ear and great craftsmanship made Marquand a valuable recorder of "his segment of the world."

He confessed once that he had never been able to write poetry or to keep rhythm in his head. And the element of poetry is missing in his work; never does he try to use this world to suggest a more ideal reality, and he does not try "To see a world in a grain of sand / And a heaven in a wild flower." His work is not designed to lift the spirit or to translate the immediate into the eternal; and he valued in other writers these same realistic qualities which he practiced. The Melville revival he recognized, but he did not share the enthusiasm of its symbol-seeking critics. Sinclair Lewis, at his best, he regarded as perhaps the major twentieth-century novelist; and he was even willing to talk with some appreciation of Booth Tarkington, although he doubted that Faulkner belonged in the company of his favorites as John Dos Passos did. In many respects he was more like Anthony Trollope than any other novelist, although he also shared many attitudes, subjects, and methods with John Galsworthy.

The actual society which he knew was his subject, and he valued it for itself, not as symbol or metaphor for transcendent truths or abstract ideals. If its manners sometimes bordered on the ridiculous, he pointed a self-conscious and mocking finger, and, while laughing, like the Thackeray of *Vanity Fair*, seemed to use the first-person plural pronoun when he thought of society, however carefully he eschewed it in writing. The puppet-master was himself always a part of the show.

There lingered over his world the sense of change, and all the wry amusement at the absurdities which that change produced could not completely mask Marquand's sense that his was an unhappy generation. Even in a late thriller like *Stopover: Tokyo* he stated his feeling that "the world was unhappy." Jack Rhyce, the protagonist, knows that "he and his generation were children of discontent." Rhyce's analysis of this discontent seems strange for a spy thriller but it states Marquand's position very clearly—more plainly, in fact, than he states it in novels of more serious import and subtler method: "All his generation had been born and nurtured in an age of discontent, but he was not able to explain the reason for it, unless that a system or a way of life was approaching dissolution. Logically there were less reasons for unhappiness today in any part of the world than there had been fifty years before. The cleavage between wealth and poverty had been greater then, and the voice of social conscience had only been a whisper. Communication and industrial advance had been negligible compared with the present, and so had public health and expectancy of life; yet back in that harder day the world had been much happier. There had been security then in that everyone knew what to expect. There had been strength and order, which perhaps were the attributes that mankind most desired." But he knew, too, that the past had had its problems, frustrations, and defeats. The mood that overshadows his Vanity Fair, like that of Thackeray's, is "Ah! *Vanitas Vanitatum!* Which of us is happy in this world? Which of us has his desire? or, having it, is satisfied?"

Maxwell Geismar once said, "Mr. Marquand knows all the little answers. He avoids the larger questions." The statement, although true in a sense, is more witty than wise. Denied the soaring reaches of transcendental thought or poetic elevation, he dealt with the little answers in large part because the people of whom he wrote were people who asked little questions of life, except in those confused moments when they merely raised frightened cries. Gertrude Stein, just before she died, asked, "What is the answer?" Receiving no reply, she laughed and said, "In that case, what is the question?" Marquand's people really never face the nature of their existence, even in dying. Perhaps the harshest thing that can be said about them is that they don't know what the larger questions truly are and, unlike Miss Stein, never ask. In *Women and Thomas Harrow*, Marquand says, "most of mankind (excepting always those who were helped by psychoanalysts . . .) never knew where they were going until they got there; and when you were there, you could never find a backward turn."

The life, world, and times of these people who are so obsessed with the material trivia of their daily deeds, the stifling formulas of their caste and class, the busyness of making money, and the confused personal diplomacy which their marriages demand are indeed unflattering but very amusing pictures of ourselves. The claim can be made for Marquand that he examined the social condition of our lives with irony and grace, and his "badgered American male" captures in his recurrent problems and poses, not only how we behave, but also how hollow our lives often are at the core. He speaks both to our social historical sense and to the unslacked spiritual thirst which our aridity creates. To our age, at least, he speaks with ease and skill, with irony and wit, but above all with the authority of unsentimental knowledge.

April in Queenborough

ELLEN GLASGOW'S COMEDIES OF MANNERS

In Ellen Glasgow was imbedded the rebellious yoking of two incompatible traditions and attitudes toward life. "I had the misfortune . . . to inherit a long conflict of types," she said in 1943, "for my father was a descendant of Scottish Calvinists and my mother a perfect flower of the Tidewater, in Virginia. Her ancestors had been broad Church of England and later agnostics. This conflict began in my soul as far back as I can remember." She spent her youth and young womanhood in open, angry, and often anguished rebellion against the darkness of her father's grim Presbyterian world, and, it seems from her revealing, fascinating, romantic—and, perhaps, romanticized—autobiography, *The Woman Within*, identified herself almost pathologically with her mother and with her mother's Tidewater world and her mother's wrongs.

Between 1897 and 1922 she wrote thirteen novels in which she pursued the ideals of realism and instructed the world in what she was learning from Darwin, Henry George, Schopenhauer, Nietzsche, and the Fabian socialists, among whom she counted herself. Up to the age of forty-nine, her life, aside from this realm of thought and creativity, had been one of ill-health, growing deafness, suffering, bereavement, anger, unhappy love affairs, humiliation, and despair—or at least, looking back upon it, she saw it so. But after 1922, after she was reconciled to the end of her engagement to Henry Anderson, she found herself in what she later called "one of those blessed pauses that fall between the 'dark wood' of the soul and the light on the horizon." In that blessed pause she did almost all her best work, and she was certainly correct when she said, "Between fifty and sixty I lived perhaps my fullest and richest years." During those years she produced *Barren Ground* and the three Queenborough novels—*The Romantic Comedians*, *They Stooped to Folly*, and *The Sheltered Life*. She explained this success to J. Donald Adams: "So long as I was held fast in the toils of life, suffering within my own ego, it was impossible to project my whole self into my novels"—by which, I submit, she really meant "keep my whole self in large part out of my novels."

She declared late in life that she ended her history of manners in Virginia with *Life and Gabriella*—conveniently forgetting those two failures, *The Builders* and *One Man in His Time*. With *Barren Ground*, she said, "I broke away from social history." *Barren Ground* was also the book in which she rediscovered and understood at least the secular implications of her father's dark Calvinism, seeing behind its theological symbols a pragmatic truth about life—the grim philosophy of fortitude, which despite her angry and tearful rejection she could finally no more escape than could Thomas Carlyle or Nathaniel Hawthorne or Herman Melville.

Into the story of Dorinda Oakley she could pour herself—perhaps with too few restraints. "If falling in love could be bliss, I discovered presently," she wrote in *The Woman Within*, "that falling out of love could be blissful tranquillity." She heaped upon Dorinda her suffering, her bitterness, her sense, as James Branch Cabell put it, of "the outrageous unfairness of heaven's traffic with Ellen Glasgow," and then she gave Dorinda the victory. At the end of the novel she wrote: "The storm and the hag-ridden dreams of the night were over, and the land which she had forgotten was waiting to take her back to its heart. Endurance. Fortitude. The spirit of the land was flowing into her, and her own spirit, strengthened and refreshed, was flowing out again toward life. . . . This was what remained to her after the years had taken their bloom. She would find happiness again. Not the happiness for which she had once longed, but the serenity of mind which is above the conflict of frustrated desires." If this is overwriting, it is—like much of her overwriting—the result not of overexpressing or sentimentalizing Dorinda but of speaking too plainly and strongly for herself.

Barren Ground was a critical success, and in the serene mood which followed it—"I wrote *Barren Ground*," she said, "and immediately I knew I had found myself"—she was ready to do her best work. "I always wanted to put my best into my books— to make them compensate, in a way for . . . the long tragedy of my life," she wrote Stark Young. "The only thing I have saved out of the wreck is the gift of work." The gift of work was enough. Out of "the tranquil immunity of a mind that had finished with love" and that had come to honor the tragic virtue of fortitude, she was to fashion the Queenborough novels before the pendulum of the conflict continued its swing until her dark vein of iron took total command.

Always she had borne—silently and in the novelist's way—a didactic burden. Her novels had been instructive exempla through which she taught her place and region the error of its ways or explored and assuaged the ache of her own disasters. Now in the serene and tranquil autumn of her life, she seems almost instinctively to have discovered a release from the didactic burden, and in that release to have found in the comedy of manners a form in which she could utilize her skill, her wit, her concern with style, her deep-rooted insider's knowledge of Virginia aristocracy, and her slowly developed novelistic skill to their best advantage. The force in the lifelong conflict between her father who "was of Valley stock and Scottish in every nerve and sinew" (as she said) and her Tidewater mother had seemingly reached an equilibrium in this calm time between her fifty-second and her sixtieth years. The equilibrium, of course, was unstable, for the harsh world of her father was to grow in strength and find its expression in her celebration of endurance in *Vein of Iron*, which she defined admiringly in 1935 as the "Scottish strain for fortitude that has come down from the earliest pioneers in the Valley," and finally in the gathering darkness of *In This Our Life*.

In 1926, weary from the three-year struggle with *Barren Ground*, Miss Glasgow felt, she says, "the comic spirit . . . struggle against the bars of its cage. . . . It was thirsting, as I was, for laughter; but it craved delicate laughter with ironic echoes." In this mood she embarked on *The Romantic Comedians* (1926), wrote it quickly, and then followed it with *They Stooped to Folly* (1929), and completed what she recognized as a trilogy with *The Sheltered Life* (1932). Over the three novels hovers the comic spirit and a conscious delight. "The last thing I wished to do," she said, "was to transfix the wings of my comic spirit. . . . For I had come at last to perceive, after my long apprenticeship to veracity, that the truth of art and the truth of life are two different truths." The completed trilogy she called "The Tragicomedy of Manners" and said, "These [novels] depict the place and tragicomedy of the individual in an established society. They illustrate the struggle of personality against tradition and the social background."

The comedy of manners was ideally suited to her purposes, her mood, and her art. It is a form that asks that its characters be placed in a sharply definable social situation, usually one that is elegant and sophisticated, and that the manners, beliefs, and conventions of that society be the forces that motivate the action. Its style is witty, its thrust satiric. It usually places in its fable an emphasis on the "love game" and centers on at least one pair of immoral lovers. The comedy of manners on the stage and in the novel also demands a highly developed craftsmanship and a delight taken by author and audience alike in finished artistry, in conscious and successful artifice. That definition describes each of the novels in the Queenborough trilogy and the trilogy as a whole, although there is a steady deepening of the seriousness and broadening of the scope of the books as the trilogy progresses. *The Romantic Comedians* is almost pure comedy. If there is, as she said, "tragedy in the theme," it is also, as she added, "tragedy running on light feet." In *They Stooped to Folly* the cast is larger, and the action, which is also compressed into a year, is given historical perspective, however lightly, by allowing us to see three "fallen" women living according to the social codes of three historical periods. Thus the past, which is only a faint reference point in *The Romantic Comedians*, assumes more depth and takes on a tinkling reso-

nance in *They Stooped to Folly*. This deepening seriousness
continues to grow in *The Sheltered Life*, where the action covers more than eight years but reaches backward in time to set
Queenborough and its aristocrats against a pattern of southern
history extending back before the Civil War. The seriousness of
the issues at stake has also intensified. The unhappiness of December unwisely wedded to May, which had all the lightness of
Restoration comedy in *The Romantic Comedians*, has deepened into issues that now literally are matters of life and death.
Yet, as I shall try to show, all three novels are truly comedies;
none is fundamentally tragic, and over them all echoes the silvery laughter of Meredith's comic spirit.

To appreciate fully both Miss Glasgow's accomplishment
and the comic implications of the Queenborough novels, it is
necessary to look at her role as narrator. For, however much
the three novels vary, Ellen Glasgow remains remarkably consistent as their teller. Everywhere she is present: although she
has learned most of the lessons of point of view and authorial
effacement which the realists taught—particularly those of
Henry James, for whom she actually had only a qualified liking
—they are lessons that she suited to her own purposes.

Louis D. Rubin once observed: "It is a good rule of thumb for
the Glasgow novels that whenever the author begins identify-
ing a character's plight with her own, begins projecting her
personal wishes and needs into the supposedly fictional situation, then to that extent both the character and the novel are
weakened." Looking at it from a different direction, Louis Auchincloss said: "She was unable sufficiently to pull the tapestry
of fiction over her personal grievances and approbations. The
latter are always peeping out at the oddest times and in the
oddest places." These observations are generally true of the early
novels, and they are particularly true of *Barren Ground*. Always in the fourteen novels before *The Romantic Comedians*,
Miss Glasgow had personal and emotional involvements with
one or more of her characters, who spoke as her surrogates and
through whom she achieved vicarious solutions to the torment-
ing problems to which she was victim in life. In these novels

from time to vexing time the thin but essential line between the author's actuality and the fictional world she created was crossed, as it was to be in the novels of Thomas Wolfe. In a discussion of the implied author in which he cites *Barren Ground* as an illustration of authorial intrusion, Louis Rubin reminds us that "it is not the narrative's fidelity to truth as such that the reader of a novel must be made to accept, but rather the storyteller's fidelity to the story."

Ellen Glasgow's great accomplishment in the Queenborough novels is that her stance as implied author is always outside the action of the stories she tells, although she tells them with an insider's sure, affectionate, but by no means gentle satiric knowledge. Yet, like the puppet-master role that Thackeray assumes toward audience and actors in *Vanity Fair*, her attitude is clear, her presence is authoritatively felt, and her persistent irony is a function of style and of her defining for us, without crossing the line between the fact of personal experience and the fiction of imagination, a reality against which the appearances of the novels are to be seen. It should come as a surprise to no one who has studied the Queenborough novels that she considered *Tom Jones* the "best of all English and American novels."

In the Queenborough novels Ellen Glasgow was given the grace to view her characters with the disinterestedness of a creator rather than to suffer with them as surrogates of her anguished self. And this quality allowed her to use her intimate knowledge of an ordered and mannered society without self-service, to re-create her world like a true Maker, and in its gravest moments to flood it with the silvery laughter of Meredithian comedy. Even in the darkening close of *The Sheltered Life*, the author seems to stand without, above, removed, like dead Troilus in Chaucer's *Troilus and Criseyde*, in "the hollowness of the eighth sphere," who

> . . . down from that high station . . . began
> To look upon this little spot of earth
> Enfolded by the sea, with full contempt
> For this unhappy world . . . and at the last
> He looked down on the place where he was slain,

> And laughed within himself at all the woe
> Of those who wept and sorrowed for his death,
> Condemning all our work that so pursues
> Blind lusts that cannot last.

Ellen Glasgow, in her role as narrator or implied author, maintains a figurative distance quite as great as Troilus's literal one.

Out of this distance and her skill and style emerges a very self-conscious yet effective artifice, so that the Queenborough novels are consciously *written* novels, and a part of their success rests upon our delight—a delight common to most high comedy —in the artificer joyfully at work at her hard-earned, highly wrought craft. (And, in an aside to the current biographers appalled at the way she ordered and designed her life and her career, one might add that it is possible to see that ordering too as a triumph of the artificer over reluctant materials, of the will over fate.)

We can sum up the Queenborough novels as the comedy of the missed delight, the hunger for the unknown timeless instant of joy, the sorrow of the aged for the passing of what Chaucer called "the blinde lust, the which that may not laste." Martin Seymour-Smith, in a gross oversimplification, says of Ellen Glasgow that she had "the limiting view that consists of specifically sexual disappointment followed by stoical acceptance." Certainly in novels before *The Romantic Comedians* we see that pattern appearing regularly, and it continues in the Queenborough novels. And in them, too, although they are novels of age rather than youth, the missed delight is directly linked with sex: hence the passage of time is portentous, and time is the great enemy for the characters. Of old General Archbald, meditating on his past life and the married English woman he had loved and lost half a century before, she said: "Like other men all over the world, he had sacrificed to gods as fragile as the bloom of light on the tulip tree. And what was time itself but the bloom, the sheath enfolding experience? Within time, and within time alone, there was life—the gleam, the quiver, the heart-beat, the immeasurable joy and anguish of being."

Actually most of the major characters in the Queenborough novels fall into one of two groups: the old who remember, long, regret, and are sad; and the young who declare their right to their own lives and will almost certainly lose them. To see such persons in such potentially tragic situations as figures in a comedy requires, as Troilus had, a vantage point in space or philosophy from which they are viewed. For Ellen Glasgow that vantage point was essentially her father's dark belief, a view of civilization, and a sense of the triviality of hedonism. I think there is no need to argue that Ellen Glasgow is speaking her own view rather than Mrs. Upchurch's (in *The Romantic Comedians*), when she refers to Mrs. Upchurch's "conventional mind [which] preferred to hold a world war, rather than original sin, responsible for Annabel's misguided behaviour." She seemed to be applauding when General Archbald, in *The Sheltered Life*, declared that "mankind was still calling human nature a system and trying vainly to put something in its place." It is the author who, in *The Romantic Comedians,* concludes that "a symbol [Duty] . . . is better than an abyss to fall back upon." And when the young fling themselves eagerly upon the sword of the first world war, General Archbald concludes with a wryness that is certainly Miss Glasgow's that "what the world needed . . . was the lost emblem of evil." When, in *A Certain Measure*, she refers to the world of *The Sheltered Life* as "a shallow and aimless society of happiness-hunters, who lived in a perpetual flight from reality, and grasped at any effort-saving illusion of passion or pleasure," it is the portion of herself incubated in Scotland, nurtured in the Valley of Virginia, and trained by her Presbyterian father that is speaking.

In fact the view she expressed of civilization is one that puts its pretenses to serious test. "The wonder in every age," General Archbald (whom she declared in the preface to be "a lover of wisdom, a humane and civilized soul") supposed, "was not that most men were savage, but that a few men were civilized." He later qualified even this limited optimism saying, "a Red Indian lurks in every man we call civilized." Curle Littlepage, in *They Stooped to Folly*, was, Miss Glasgow said, a man who "may make the world a desert and call it progress." And his father, Virginius Littlepage, brooded over the modern world in these terms: "Modern life especially appeared without dignity and even without direction, an endless speeding to nowhere." She characterized civilization as immature: "In America," she said, "the cult of the immature had prevailed over the order of merit," and she condemned what she called "the worship of adolescents and other myths of primitive culture."

When she moved from this larger frame of beliefs to the small, dry, and dying aristocratic world of Queenborough, the dislike of its values became intense. Of Queenborough she said, "I felt that I required the distilled essence of all Virginia cities rather than the speaking likeness of one"; yet, declaring her freedom from the bondage of literal fact, she said, "I have not failed . . . to make two trees grow in my Queenborough where only one was planted before me in Richmond," so Richmond was clearly and recognizably in her mind. (It is tempting to play with the name Queenborough: the queen is certainly Elizabeth the Virgin Queen, so Queenborough is Virginia City, which is Richmond. But Queenborough is very close in sound to Queensberry, and the Marquis of Queensberry's rules are very precise regulations strictly governing a conflict, a boxing match: hence the name suggests very formal and stylized rules of conduct.) This Queenborough was committed to "evasive idealism that had become a second nature . . . to the whole community"; it existed in "an epoch when faith and facts did not cultivate an acquaintance." Like Mrs. Upchurch, it "was natural only when it was artificial." It tried to create a "sheltered life," a "smiling region of phantasy," but its smile was often like that animated grimace of Eva Birdsong's, which finally settled into a rictus. Like Judge Honeywell and "like most lawyers and all vestrymen, [it] was able to believe automatically a number of things that [it] knew were not true." It existed as an interlocking protectorate of families, which might disapprove, as General Archbald knew, but would rally around a member through clan loyalty: "All the old families that were not rotten within would close round him [if he supported his granddaughter's marriage to a plain man], just as they would close round him if he had forged a cheque or murdered his uncle"; as, indeed, they had rallied round the Goddards, who "had united in the heroic pretense that plain murder was pure accident. By force of superior importance, they had ignored facts, defended family honour, shielded a murderer for the sake of saving a name, turned public execration into sympathy, and politely but firmly looked the law out of countenance." The special gift of Queenborough society was its "capacity to believe anything or nothing," to subordinate happiness, even love, to pride, to make the highest art of conversation and appearance. Ellen Glasgow says: "Even in Queenborough, where until recent years, conversation had been the favourite and almost the only art patronized by the best circles, wealthy citizens were beginning to realize that, if books look well in a library, pictures lend even more emphatically the right note in decoration to the walls of a drawing room." Using this view of the world and this attitude toward a decaying Virginia aristocracy, Ellen Glasgow in the Queenborough novels made a cool, detached presentation of the world she knew best, loved sincerely, and had an amused and tolerant contempt for.

Fundamental to her artistry was the choice of her narrative point of view. In all three novels she elected the same basic approach, and it is one that is markedly Jamesian in concept. She elected to report, essentially through the witty and epigrammatic voice of the implied author, that aspect of the consciousness of major characters which is capable of being verbalized directly. Each of the novels begins with a long and unbroken presentation of such a center of consciousness. The first ten chapters of *The Romantic Comedians* (a little over one-third of the book) are a report of the thoughts and feelings of Judge Gamaliel Honeywell, but those thoughts, although presented directly, have passed through the alembic of Ellen Glasgow's skillful and sometimes scornful reporting. In a typical remark that "he had been happy with Cordelia, as a man may be happy in a marriage with any agreeable woman when he stops thinking about it," we hear a direct witty interpretation by the implied author. It is difficult for a thoughtful and remembering reader ever to overcome the effect of such reporting as this statement: "It is astonishing, he reflected, with the slow but honourable processes of the judicial mind, what Spring can do to one even at sixty-five—even at a young sixty-five, he hastened to remind himself." This distance and this tone well established, Miss Glasgow then begins in the eleventh chapter to shift the point of view to the consciousness of other characters —Annabel, Mrs. Upchurch, and Amanda; and it shifts often, frequently for ironic effect.

In *They Stooped to Folly* the first third is centered with equal force and much the same effect in the consciousness of Virginius Littlepage. The second third is predominantly, although not exclusively, in the consciousness of his wife, Victoria, but the consciousnesses of other characters also are entered from time to time. The last third moves freely among the consciousnesses of several characters, quite clearly for ironic contrast. In the concluding chapter of Part First, for example, we are told of Virginius's "sense of universal futility" that "joy he had never known in its fulness. He had had his years or his seasons, but never his moments." Were it not for Ellen Glasgow's style and the dry wit of her reporting, the sympathy that we naturally feel for Littlepage might almost have moved to the sentimental, if not the maudlin. But should style have surrendered temporarily to sentiment, it could not long remain in that position. Six thousand words later we are in the consciousness of his wife, sorrowing in the memory that Virginius had been Virginius rather than "the young Lochinvar of her mind" and that "she had missed some finer essence of living, some purer distillation of joy." If—as I doubt—Ellen Glasgow is saying, "Oh, the pity of it all!" she is saying it not in tears but in laughter. This principle of ironic juxtaposition—one of her basic comic devices—is well illustrated by two sections late in the novel. In one, at the end of chapter 7, Louisa Goddard reflects on the changes which she considers improvements: "Nothing was worth all the deceit, all the anguish, all the futile hope and ineffectual endeavor, all the pretense and parade, all the artificial glamour and empty posturing of the great Victorian tradition." In the following three pages, Virginius is sorrowful over the loss of "the true feminine character which had never flowered more perfectly than in the sheltered garden of the Southern tradition." The posture the implied author is asking the reader to assume is not with either Virginius or Louisa but above them and superior in knowledge and insight to either.

In the preface to *The Sheltered Life* she wrote in 1938, from the deepening despair of her later years, about a comedy which she considered one of her two best books (the other was *Barren Ground*), but she placed an emphasis on its tragic qualities at the expense of its comedy, leading to a series of later critical distortions. If the book is not comedy, as I think it is, then the alternative is not tragedy—the people lack stature and the action lacks significance—but pathos and sentimentality. In the preface she describes the form of the book as a function of point of view: "In *The Sheltered Life*, where I knew intuitively that the angle of vision must create the form, I employed two points of view alone. . . . Age and youth look on the same scene, the same persons, the same events. . . . Between these conflicting points of view the story flows on, as a stream flows in a narrow valley. Nothing happens that is not seen, on one side, through the steady gaze of the old man, seeing life as it is, and, on the other side, by the troubled eyes of the young girl, seeing life as she would wish it to be." The first of the three parts, "The Age of Make-Believe," is told through the consciousness of Jenny Blair Archbald, aged nine going on ten. The second part, "The Deep Past," is General Archbald's recollection of the past—a section of which Miss Glasgow said in 1944, "'The Deep Past' contains the writing I should wish to be remembered by in the future," a judgment in which most of her critics join her. The long third part, "The Illusion," alternates between Jenny and the general. Certainly parts 2 and 3 succeed as well as anything Ellen Glasgow ever wrote. The weakness in the book—and I consider it weak in structure and the least successful of the Queenborough novels—results from two facts. General Archbald is intended to be the protagonist—not merely because she so asserted to Allen Tate the year of its publication but also because that is the common structure of the Queenborough novels, as we shall see a little later. But beginning with a section located in Jenny Blair's consciousness violates the structural pattern Ellen Glasgow had established for the Queenborough novels and has led many critics to see her as the protagonist. Setting the story in motion when Jenny Blair is only nine places a heavy burden on Miss Glasgow's ironic style, with the result that in this section, almost alone among the Queenborough novels, the distance of author from character and action is uncertain. Furthermore Jenny at nine is incapable of some of the thoughts that she is assigned. I cite one example: "What was it about Mrs. Peyton, Jenny Blair asked herself, gazing at the ashen hair and the long, thin face, with its pale skin the texture of a withered rose, that made her remember a Confederate flag in the rain? She wasn't, of course, in the very least like a Confederate flag. No lady could be. Yet Jenny Blair never looked at her that she didn't think of a flag going by in the rain to the inspiring music of bands." Now this figure is a most effective one, suggesting gallantry and defeat, brave display and heartrending futile courage. It is, however, Ellen Glasgow and not Jenny Blair who is thinking it. It is one thing for the implied author to couch a character's consciousness in the author's ironic language; it is quite a different thing to give the character thoughts and insights clearly beyond her years. This is the old problem that Ellen Glasgow had had in earlier novels and notably in *Barren Ground*. Its effect here is to give the hard selfishness of Jenny Blair—whose true role is much like that of Annabel in *The Romantic Comedians* and Milly Burden in *They Stooped to Folly*—an authorial sanction that is not intended. The novel never completely recovers from the skewing of attitude that occurs in part 1. And the weakness is a function of an uncertain distance between author and subject. For a short time —enough to cast doubts but not completely to destroy illusion— Troilus descends from the eighth sphere, Ellen the Maker finds some middle ground between Olympus and earth, and the silvery laughter is muted but by no means stilled.

In fiction as consciously and meticulously constructed as the Queenborough novels, meaning is a product of structure. And the structure of each of these three novels, like the use of the Olympian implied author and of shifting centers of consciousness in them, is remarkably similar. They might be grouped as a trilogy under the common title *April in Queenborough*, for their time-settings are April, and indeed in them

> April is the cruellest month, breeding
> Lilacs out of the dead land, mixing
> Memory and desire, stirring
> Dull roots with spring rain.

The reference to T.S. Eliot is not accidental: those lines define in miniature the central fable of the Queenborough novels, and her emphasis on April cannot be accidental. The late Robert Holland examined Ellen Glasgow's work as pictures of a wasteland and Virginius Littlepage as a character much like Eliot's Prufrock. It should be remembered that she was enthusiastic about that most Eliot-like of southern poems, Allen Tate's "Ode to the Confederate Dead," which she called "a great poem, because it strips away not only appearances but experience itself, and bares some dark and nameless quality of being."

Each novel has the same basic plot situation. In Queenborough, a society of now empty and sterile forms, people in late middle or old age, who have surrendered themselves to these forms, try vainly to rebel and to achieve a previously unexperienced happiness through sexual love before it is too late. The young whom they love rebel against them, Queenborough, and their now outmoded set of values without even trying. In *The Romantic Comedians* Judge Gamaliel Honeywell, who in his youth had been in love with Amanda Lightfoot but had married Cordelia, whom he did not love, now made a widower by Cordelia's death, marries the young Annabel Upchurch in a search for lost youth; she does not love him and finally leaves him. In *They Stooped to Folly* a successful, middle-aged lawyer, Virginius Littlepage, has had a successful but dull and unimpassioned marriage to Victoria, and now dreams of an affair with Mrs. Dalrymple, of sullied reputation and generous curves, but finally lacks the courage to realize it. His sister Agatha, a ruined woman of the Victorian era, still stays upstairs in disgrace. His secretary Milly Burden has had a child out of wedlock by Martin Welding, whom his daughter Mary Victoria has married but who leaves her. Remorseless Milly is seeking her own life. In *The Sheltered Life* young Jenny Blair Archbald falls in love with middle-aged George Birdsong, the philandering husband of her friend, the famous beauty Eva Birdsong. Her grandfather, General David Archbald, an eighty-three-year-old lawyer, who married because he had accidentally but innocently compromised a woman whom he did not love and who had lost the one woman whom he had loved because she was already married, is the contrasting center of consciousness to Jenny Blair. Eva Birdsong, who is ill, sees Jenny and George in an embrace and kills her husband.

The protagonist of each book is an elderly or aging man. Each, like General Archbald, "had longed to seek and find his one brief hour of delight." Each, like Judge Honeywell, felt "that he had missed the secret of life . . . that he had lost beyond recovery something indescribably fresh and satisfying." These men remind us of Lambert Strether of James's *The Ambassadors*, but they experience Strether's awakening to their unlived lives much later than James's protagonist does. They are now at or close to old age, and they have sacrificed youth, middle age, dreams, imagination, and vital instincts to "the moral earnestness of tradition." It was true of them, as Ellen Glasgow wrote of Asa Timberlake in *In This Our Life*: "For the sake of a past tradition he had spent nearly thirty years doing things he hated and not doing things he liked; and at the end of that long self-discipline, when he was too old to begin over again, he had seen his code of conduct flatten out and shrivel up as utterly as a balloon that is pricked." Each in his own way shared Judge Honeywell's "natural aptitude for evading unpleasant truths." Each, like Virginius Littlepage, had a "hidden flaw in his nature which made it harder for him to commit a pleasure than to perform a duty, which made him hesitate and fail in the hour of adventure." Jenny Blair reports accurately of General Archbald: "Mamma told me he was so queer when he was young that everybody was surprised when he made a good living. I asked him about that and he laughed and said that he made a good living by putting an end to himself." It is easy enough to see in these protagonists aspects of Ellen Glasgow's life and attitudes about which she could on occasion be almost lugubriously self-pitying. But here they are used—not as personal experience but as transmuted material for fiction—not as a basis for tragedy or self-pity but for genial comedy.

Each of the novels also has a collection of women who are embodiments of the tradition of Queenborough, often in its most admirable form. The wives Cordelia Honeywell, Victoria Littlepage, and Erminia Archbald are capable, practical, intelligent, and devoted women; and each contributes enormously to her husband's success and ease of living, if not to his happiness. Only Victoria Littlepage is alive during the forward action of one of the books, and she is one of the triumphs of *They Stooped to Folly.* There is a comic poignance to her being shown to have the same regrets and unfulfilled dreams of ecstasy as Virginius has. In each there is an embodiment of tradition in the form of a lost romance: Amanda Lightfoot, who remains faithful to Judge Honeywell; Mrs. Dalrymple, who beckons to Mr. Littlepage's dreams of joy, and Louisa Goddard, who has loved him silently all these years; Eva Birdsong, the model of beauty, sacrifice, and fidelity to George and to General Archbald, and the English woman whom Archbald briefly and passionately loved in his youth. There are other middle-aged widows, who represent the society and dominate the men of their world: Mrs. Upchurch, the cheerful pragmatist; Mrs. Burden, committed to the lower middle-class prejudices; Mrs. Archbald, the general's efficient daughter-in-law. There were also women in each novel whose lives were sacrificed to the tradition: Amanda Lightfoot, Agatha Littlepage, and Etta Archbald. This society of Queenborough is a thoroughly feminine world, dominated by wives, aunts, mothers, and daughters. It is they who have shaped for each of the protagonists a world such as that of General Archbald, of whom Ellen Glasgow said: "He had had a fair life. Nothing that he wanted, but everything that was good for him." But good though the life they make for the protagonists is, Ellen Glasgow was not gentle with them. Mrs. Archbald she accused of "persevering hypocrisy . . . the triumph of self-discipline" and said, "Even her realm of phantasy was a small, enclosed province, peopled by skeletons of tradition and governed by a wooden theology." Of Eva Birdsong, considered by some critics an admirable character, she was particularly and devastatingly severe: "She had never drawn a natural breath since she was married," and Miss Glasgow told us that Eva did not work in the garden or love flowers, that she preferred hot-house plants, and that she never wanted a child. She is as sterile, lifeless, and artificial as the dazzling smile which she could turn on as though by a switch. Only toward Victoria was Ellen Glasgow kindly.

Of crucial importance in each of the Queenborough novels is a young girl who is modern, headstrong, hedonistic, and selfish, and around whom the action of the novel revolves. These young girls are startlingly alike in character and attitude. Jenny Blair Archbald speaks for them all when she declares, "All I want to do is to live my own life." Milly Burden gives the wish an Emersonian twist when she says, "I shouldn't consent to take my experience from you second hand." Ellen Glasgow says, "The actual boundary between youth and age is the moment when one realizes that one cannot change life." These modern young ladies are far from that line.

It seems plain to me that these novels are intimately related and mutually complementary ironic portraits of the same hedonistic society, judged against the serious, even grim standards of Ellen Glasgow's later years. That they are comedies, albeit quiet ones, is a result of attitude, tone, and style. The implied author of the Queenborough novels gained for Ellen Glasgow a fortunate freedom for wit and epigram. She has often been criticized for a tendency of her style to intrude on her narratives, but the Maker and Voice of Queenborough has a defined position from which she can exercise her gift for wit and epigram freely. In 1928, writing of *The Romantic Comedians* and while *They Stooped to Folly* was in the press and *The Sheltered Life* was getting under way, she said: "The style of writing was what I gave most thought to from the first page to the last." The Queenborough novels are loaded with epigrams, such as: "Necessity is the reluctant mother of endurance." "Edmonia had been born with the courage of her appetites." "Mrs. Upchurch . . . had a small mind but knew it thoroughly." "Her ideas were so correct that it was sometimes difficult for her to make conversation." "The worst of all possible worlds would be one invented by good women." "The virtue of perfect behavior lies, not in its rightness, but in its impenetrability." "That prevalent class which our rude ancestors dismissed as scatterbrains, but which superior persons today cherish as intelligentsia." "The Judge was tolerant of any views that were not brought into vocal conflict with his own." "A mind so sprightly that it was not troubled by convictions." "The long Victorian age . . . when womanhood was exalted from a biological fact into a miraculous power." Mr. Littlepage's father "had found it less embarrassing to commit adultery than to pronounce the word in the presence of a lady." "It really takes two to make an influence." "Poor Aunt Agatha had fallen like a perfect lady." Mr. Littlepage was reconciled to a war "that diverted Mary Victoria's mission from the Congo, where faces were incurably black, to the Balkan kingdoms, where, he charitably assumed, they were merely sallow." "Judge Honeywell, whose faith, however flexible, was triumphant over logic (who could recite the Apostles' Creed so long as he was not required to practise the Sermon on the Mount, and could countenance Evolution until it threatened the image of its Maker)." "Though a trifle heavy in figure, she [Isabella] was nimble in mind and vivacious in conversation, a little too wide for the sheath skirt which was just going out, and not quite broad enough for the modern ideas which were just coming in." As every reader of Ellen Glasgow knows, such a group of epigrams could easily be tripled or quadrupled from any single one of the Queenborough novels. The voice here is plainly that of Ellen the Maker, indirectly telling us what opinions we should have about her characters and their world and actions. In one sense the pleasure that we take in these comedies of manners is a direct result of our participation with her in her delight at the happy exercise of her urbane craft. What finally lingers longest in our minds after we read the Queenborough novels is this invisible and omnipresent Maker —sophisticated, detached, amused, gently satiric—fashioning the world she knows best into a comic object.

The line between comedy and tragedy is definite but paradoxically indefinable. It helps, perhaps, to say, as Walter Kerr does, that tragedy is the record of man's struggle to realize his ultimate capabilities, the reflection of his nobility of spirit and the magnitude of his possible action, and that comedy is the record of his limitations, the restraints of the frail flesh, the blind lusts of the mighty. It is in her record of such limitations that the people of Queenborough—good and wise, like General Archbald; weak and foolish, like Virginius Littlepage; trapped and frantic, like Eva Birdsong; or self-serving and adolescent, like Jenny Blair—live. And it is in the definition of such limitations imposed by society and human weakness upon the self that Ellen Glasgow is most truly a writer of comedy.

In his tone poem *Ein Heldenleben* Richard Strauss dramatizes the life of his hero from the early days of arrogant defiance, through the hard struggle for recognition, into the great battles for victory, then in the calm triumph of success, and, finally into a period of quiet peace. In the next to the last section—the period of late middle age, of success—Strauss used recapitulations of his own great tone poems to suggest the garnering of the victor's laurels. It seems to me that Ellen Glasgow's career follows a quite similar structure. In her early career she defied the household gods of her Virginia aristocracy; in her middle years she struggled through to personal and artistic success against great handicaps and harsh events; in the sixth decade of her life, having won a victory at a high cost, she moved into a serene and tranquil time when she could look at her subject, her life, and herself with a hard-won detachment and allow the comic spirit to dictate to her both a mood and a mode for order-

April in Queenborough

ing and recapitulating her life. It is to this period and this mood that the Queenborough novels belong; and as the clear expression of the triumph of spirit over flesh, of will over fate, of detachment over despair, and as the embodiment of a personality and a style in works of high craftsmanship, they have seldom been surpassed in the American novel of manners.

It seems to me that *The Romantic Comedians* is, as she herself immodestly asserted, unsurpassed as an American comedy of manners. It is almost without flaw—the only serious one that I can find being her failure to play out the scene in which the judge learns of Annabel's leaving him. *They Stooped to Folly* has a broader theme than *The Romantic Comedians* and is almost as perfect in execution, although it is less compact and its characters are less intimately related to a single action. *The Sheltered Life* has a theme that is deeper and a meaning that covers more of the territory of historical and moral record, but it is flawed by the weakness of the point of view at the beginning and by a tendency from time to time for Miss Glasgow to lose some of the essential detachment that never wavers in the first two of the books. But taken all in all, the Queenborough novels form a triptych of Virginia aristocratic life and manners that treats them with knowing affection and yet submits them to the gently corrosive irony of a great comic wit. They succeed admirably in that difficult and rare genre, the American comedy of manners.

Barren Ground *and the Shape of History*

B*arren Ground*, a novel of character set in Piedmont Virginia at a time—from 1894 to 1924—when few events significant in history occurred there, is informed at almost every point and given its structure and one level of its meaning from the shape of the social history of Virginia.

We have developed a habit of regarding a novel as historical only if it deals with actual historical characters or events or concerns itself with movements and occurrences significant in the history of a people or a race. This extremely narrow definition of a novel concerned with history virtually confines it to the romance of adventure. Yet the novel of history is in its truest sense, it seems to me, a work which reflects a historical dimension in the writer's imagination, so that consciously or unconsciously it is shaped significantly by the writer's sense of history and beliefs about history. For certain kinds of writers, such as Scott, Hugo, Dumas, Tolstoy, George Eliot, Faulkner, and, I believe, Ellen Glasgow, the shape of history was a powerful imaginative stimulant and a major component of the works that they produced.

To an appreciable degree, the shape of history is the shape not of individual movements but of mass societal movements. Yet individuals follow out in their private lives patterns determined at least in part by societal movements, and the shape of their private experiences often duplicates in microcosm the movements of society. Thus when we look at *Barren Ground* as a work related to the history of Virginia, we are not necessarily saying that it describes events in the history of Virginia—indeed, it does not—or that it reproduces actual historical characters—indeed, it does not—or that it is necessarily concerned with the major exterior movements of society. In this novel, however much Miss Glasgow had been fascinated by the social history of Virginia in her earlier works, she has, almost all critics agree, achieved the presentation of the interior self of an individual as the central focus of her story, so that the novel is a psychological and moral study of provincial life, a kind of anti-*Madame Bovary*. But what we mean in examining *Barren Ground* in terms of its use of history is not a denial of these characteristics, but an inquiry into how a writer whose imagination has a powerful historical dimension deals with an intensely personal, subjective, and psychologically precise character in a very long narrative.

Because I believe that in *Barren Ground* this historical dimension shapes the large form of the work and makes possible the individual story which the novel relates, I think we can safely say that *Barren Ground*, an intense novel of character, is also in a major sense a panel in Ellen Glasgow's social history of Virginia. The book gains added depth when viewed in this way. Just as those long and sonorous names in *Paradise Lost* not only contribute to the organ tones of Milton's mighty lines but also, when their precise denotations are understood, enrich on another level the meaning of the poem, so the shape of social history into which the individual's life is cast has a kind of truth for the individual. When that shape is discovered and explored it gives added depth. Thus a kind of silent resonance accrues to the work, so that the social history of Virginia may be said to illumine and deepen the character of Dorinda, and the record of Dorinda's sojourn in Piedmont Virginia finds its own direct referent in the larger social history of the region.

To see *Barren Ground* in terms of history is, in one sense, to follow its author's own comments about it, for Ellen Glasgow said that it could "be regarded logically as one of the scenes from country life in a social history of Virginia since the Civil War." She also argued, however, that the book could "be considered, with equal logic, to stand alone, as it does in my estimation, secure in its own weight and substance." And with equal force she insists that its southern landscape and its ties to special time and place are not essential to her interpretation of life in the novel. "The significance of this book, the quickening spirit, would not have varied, I believe," she said, "had I been born anywhere else." The story of Dorinda Oakley, she is arguing, is universal: "she exists wherever the spirit of fortitude has triumphed over the sense of futility. . . . The implicit philosophy may be summed up in a phrase: one may learn to live, one may even learn to live gallantly, without delight." There is little reason to question that the novel is for her and for most of its readers the story of the grim triumph of a resolute personality over the dark circumstances of life or that it shares a moral universe with Thomas Hardy's Wessex Novels or that it is independent of the southern landscape on which Miss Glasgow lavishes a great amount of loving attention in the book or that it is not dependent on the facts of southern history for its meaning.

But to tell the story of Dorinda Oakley, it was necessary that it take place in a pattern of events, that it have a structure or a shape that moved Dorinda from beginning through middle to end. Although Ellen Glasgow was not, as Blair Rouse has pointed out, a very inventive plotter, she was a careful, self-conscious writer who, she declared, "wrote always toward an end that I saw (I can imagine no other way of writing a book)." The necessary structure which she employed to tell the story of Dorinda Oakley was a structure like many she had used before. It drew its essential shape from southern history and the southern landscape, and *Barren Ground* became, therefore, a panel in her social history.

That it was factually faithful to the nature of the place and the experiences it described was not surprising. Ellen Glasgow was an instinctive realist, and she always strove for accuracy. Stanly Godbold in *Ellen Glasgow and the Woman Within* has pointed out how precise her picture of the agricultural methods of her character is. She said that she saw the community of Pedlar's Mill in terms of social class: "In *Barren Ground*, as in *The Sheltered Life*, I dealt with a community in which the vital stream was running out into shallows. Though they belonged to different classes of society, the one rural and the other urban, these two dissimilar social groups were both remnants of an older civilization, of a dying culture." Such a statement differs very little from many others she makes about the twelve other novels she discusses in *A Certain Measure*. For without being in the traditional sense a historical novelist—her only strictly historical piece of work is the early novel *The Battle-Ground*—Ellen Glasgow's work was informed throughout its course by an awareness of social history, and her fictional structures seem to have been shaped by what she senses as the nature of historical movements.

That shape becomes a pervasive formative structure in most of her novels. Even in her comedies of manners there is a sense of the nature of change produced by the flow of time, a change that is at the heart of their plots. *The Romantic Comedians* functions through the difference in ages and in life-styles of Judge Honeywell and Annabel Upchurch. *They Stooped to Folly* compares the differences in social conduct and in moral attitudes among three generations of fallen women, and *The Sheltered Life* brings to bear upon the present a pattern of judgment that grows from "the deep past" of General Archbald. In novels like *The Deliverance, The Voice of the People, The Romance of a Plain Man*, and a number of other works, the informing element of the plot is the movement through history of a continuing displacement of the aristocratic past by the rising middle classes. Miss Glasgow was quite explicit about this displacement being a central theme in her work.

Again and again she insisted that her novels constituted a consciously calculated social history of her native state. She said that as early as 1900 she had projected a series of novels that would form "a social history of Virginia from the decade before the Confederacy" and that her intention was to trace "the rise of the middle class as the dominant force in Southern democracy." The time at which she first so conceived her work has often been debated, largely as the result of James Branch Cabell's ungallant insistence in *As I Remember It* that it was he rather than she who first detected this theme in her novels, but there is little question that the theme is there, whoever detected it first. Its presence is not really remarkable. Southern writers early and late have been obsessed with history, from Simms and Kennedy to Faulkner and Warren. In Ellen Glasgow's case, the historical romance was the literary sustenance upon which she was suckled. Every Christmas of her childhood, she declared, "I received one of these perennial romances." She learned her ABC's from Scott's *Old Mortality* and was led to learn to read from hearing an aunt relate the plots of the Waverley Novels. When she first visited Scotland she said, "I felt that I had come to my home in the past, because of my childish adoration of Sir Walter." If we can cut through the derring-do and the medieval tinsel with which Scott is so often encased in our imaginations, we find that his novels create for us a special world caught in the process of historical change. Scott shows us the impact of social and political forces on ordinary people in that world; we know its social conditions, its political issues, and its psychological tensions from having vicariously experienced them. As Georg Lukács in *The Historical Novel* says, "Scott's greatness lies in his capacity to give living human embodiment to historical-social types." As Karl Kroeber in *Romantic Narrative Art* asserts, Scott's method depends on "the double perception of individual personality and social role."

Always too Ellen Glasgow was obsessed with time. "What was time itself," she asked in *The Sheltered Life*, "but the bloom, the sheath enfolding experience?" Her view of time is tied to sequence and process. In an often stimulating article in the *Southern Literary Journal,* Judy Smith Murr has argued that in *Barren Ground* and *Vein of Iron* Ellen Glasgow sees in the lives of her principal characters "the repetitious re-enactment of human history." But this basically Nietzschean view of history—a view in which each individual life replicates the endlessly repetitive pattern of human experience and the racial experience is repeated in each individual existence—is not the view of time and history which really informs the bulk of Ellen Glasgow's work. Her view is basically Hegelian, in that it sees history as process, the movement of large forces through sequences that lead to large cause-and-effect relationships. Miss Glasgow is informed on one level by the Scotch-Irish Presbyterianism of her father, a grim faith which she fought against for much of her life, but toward which she seems to have moved increasingly in her closing years. This faith contributed to her sense of history, for the movement of God's intention through history is for Calvin the basis of a great drama of vast cosmic forces. But she did not need to be religious in order to embrace Hegelianism. The Hegelian dialectic proved to be one of the most effective interpretations of history for Karl Marx, who certainly was to some degree an influence on Miss Glasgow's social attitudes; Marx, too, saw history as a vast drama of class conflicting with class and moving inexorably toward an inevitable conclusion. This Hegelian view of history, however, she could have learned in many ways. Scott, as Georg Lukács has pointed out, was informed by it throughout his career, and the South has been receptive to an Hegelian rather that the prevalent national Nietzschean view of history for the last hundred and fifty years, as I have tried to show in *The Immoderate Past*. I am not trying to suggest that when Miss Glasgow wrote a novel like *Barren Ground* she set out consciously to produce a parable of Virginia social history. I am confident that she did not. I am trying to suggest that whenever she turned to fiction her firmly held view of Virginia social history was so strong that it tended to give a shape to the work which she produced.

In this sense the plot of *Barren Ground* is a retelling of the history of the region in which it is set, a retelling in which the characters play representative roles. In this respect, Ellen Glasgow is not notably different from William Faulkner, for her characters tend to become, though far less passionately presented, the equivalents of Faulkner's "avatars"—that is, figures who embody or represent principles or forces in human history or experience or microcosmic embodiments of the macrocosmic shape of history and events. Faulkner was illuminating in his comments on such a method. On one occasion he said, "I discovered that my own little postage stamp of native soil was worth writing about and that I would never live long enough to exhaust it, and by sublimating the actual into the apocalyptic I

123

would have complete liberty to use whatever talent I might have to its absolute top." His characters are not symbolic, but representative, for they stand for the class of things of which they are themselves literally a part. Malcolm Cowley has observed of *The Sound and the Fury*, "Its principal theme is the decline of the Compson family, which stands by synecdoche (not symbolism) for the Old South." In *Light in August* Joe Christmas *represents* the southern white racist's fear of race; Gail Hightower becomes a type of all the inheritors of the noble southern tradition of honor and chivalry who are lost in its distorted memory and its destructive worship; Joanna Burden becomes an avatar of the liberal whose approach to the racial problem is degrading to those whose salvation she attempts to secure. Yet *Light in August* is not a parable, and its theme is not primarily sociological or political.

The characters of *Barren Ground*, in a similar way, become avatars or representatives of social classes intermingled in the complex patterns of southern history. Thus Dorinda Oakley is the product of Scotch-Irish Presbyterians who had moved down into a mythical community with marked similarities to Louisa County, which Ellen Glasgow knew well as a child. She belongs to a class that Ellen Glasgow calls "good people," as distinguished from the aristocratic "good families." The first chapter of the novel traces the racial and class history of Eudora Abernethy, Dorinda's mother and the wife of Joshua Oakley, her father, land-poor people who owned 1,000 acres and farmed it by destructive and outmoded methods and were desperately poor but without being poor whites. Jason Greylock, Dorinda's lover and betrayer, the son of the degenerate local physician, represents another element and a different class from that of Dorinda, a class to whom the people of Pedlar's Mill should have been able to look for guidance, aid, and models. But the Greylocks betray the trust placed upon them. "His breed," Miss Glasgow said in *A Certain Measure* "unlike Dorinda's, held no immunity from the fatal germ of resignation." And he "surrendered through an inherited weakness." The model and, indeed, the safeguard and protection of the people

124

of Pedlar's Mill, though also the butt of their humor and the subject of their jokes, was Nathan Pedlar, storekeeper, possessor of all the virtues of orderliness, commitment, and dedication, and who was selflessly in love with Dorinda. She uses him cruelly as her husband in that unconsummated marriage, and it is only in his death, where he is symbolically giving himself in rescuing others, that he begins to assume a role in the communal imagination that is in some way equivalent to the role which he had played in the community's lives.

Dorinda, after she is betrayed by Jason, goes to New York City, and there she gains the knowledge and skill and secures the financial means which she brings back to Pedlar's Mill and uses to redeem the wasted land and make it bloom again like a garden. She applies to the world ravaged by weather and the aftermath of the Civil War the knowledge she has gained in the North, and she becomes the dominant and the saving element in her society. When Jason's farm becomes her possession, and she rescues his drunken self from the poor farm, her revenge is complete. Though she finds great difficulty in setting aside the passionate involvement with Jason which had been at the center of her life and which dries up her capacity for love and much of her capacity for humanity, she is sustained by what Ellen Glasgow calls the "vein of iron," the quality of fortitude and perseverance which is peculiarly a product of the Presbyterian faith in the grim lives of the good people of Virginia. It proves to be the force that is able to convert a conquered land into a workable world.

Almost from the beginning of her career, Miss Glasgow had been fascinated by the forces necessary to reclaim the ruined land and build a new society upon it. In the early romantic novel *The Battle-Ground*, she had seen these qualities manifested in the aristocratic hero, Dan Montjoy, who had learned suffering and the value of simple people in the Civil War, and who came back to the ruined land to try to reestablish some order on it. In that novel, Miss Glasgow did not represent these needs through dramatized fictional presentation so much as talk about them, for she was a very young novelist still learning her craft. She says of Montjoy, as he returns from the war, "The worst was what came afterward, the sense of utter failure and the attempt to shape one's self to brutal necessity. In the future that opened before him he saw only a terrible patience which would perhaps grow into a second nature as the years went on." In another place she says with almost equal directness, "With his youth, his strength, his very bread thrown into the scales, he sat now with wrecked body and blighted mind, and saw his future turn to decay before his manhood was well begun. . . . Yes, this was the end, and he meant to face it standing with his back against the wall." In a far less dramatic sense but equally vigorously and courageously, Dorinda Oakley is essentially the same person drawn twenty-five years later, a character who brings to bear upon the task of reclaiming her world the same qualities of endurance, self-sacrifice, and fortitude.

Miss Glasgow had explored extensively the nature of the rise of people from the lower classes to the control of society in what I believe to be one of her better but most neglected novels, *The Romance of a Plain Man*. In it Ben Starr, beginning at the lowest level of society, works his way into positions of increasing strength and importance in the social, economic, and political structure of the state, yet he remains so entranced, so thoroughly in awe of the idea of a proud and aristocratic society represented by a girl whom he loves, marries, and feels that he must continually prove himself worthy of, that he is finally unable to function with true effectiveness or to have a good or a happy life. Here, too, the triumph of the rising middle classes, Miss Glasgow's major historical theme, was represented as a necessary and inevitable thing but one which brought anything but happiness to the people of that rising middle class who succeeded. In her first novel dealing with Virginia social history, *The Voice of the People*, she had shown Nick Burr, who rises from a poor street urchin to become the governor of the state and who does many good things in his career, meeting at last an unmerited death. The pattern of Dorinda's life, which can be explained and has been in many different ways, ranging from feminist admiration to Freudian excoriation, differs hardly at all from the recurrent patterns of upward-striving middle-class characters in Ellen Glasgow's earlier work.

Ellen Glasgow's use of "good people" in *Barren Ground* is very much like Faulkner's use of such people in *Light in August,* in which Lena Grove and Byron Bunch, representing the simple people, are the embodiment of the hope of the future for Yoknapatawpha County and Mississippi, and in which Gail Hightower, the ineffectual aristocrat, represents both the long betrayal of these people and of his own ideals by his spineless resignation to the false dreams of the past. Dorinda is, in certain respects, not unlike Lena Grove, and Byron Bunch is a far happier Nathan Pedlar, while Jason Greylock plays the historical role which Faulkner assigns to Gail Hightower. In the Snopes Trilogy Faulkner portrayed the triumph of the lowest classes against the aristocratic order and expressed his deep revulsion for the moral chaos which followed that displacement. One of the great differences between Miss Glasgow's view of southern history and Faulkner's is that, however much her fastidious taste was offended by certain aspects of the rising middle class, she did not view that rise as a tragedy or look upon it as being without hope, or see it as purely materialistic and destructive of the old values. Faulkner was much more wedded to the ideals of his aristocratic families than Ellen Glasgow was, however much she admired, loved, and mocked them.

What I am trying to suggest here, is that when Ellen Glasgow came to write what is perhaps her most personal and autobiographical novel, *Barren Ground,* she embodied in Dorinda Oakley many of her own emotions and experiences and celebrated in Dorinda those qualities which she believed she most admirably had. Yet it was necessary for her to place that character in a story, a fable, and the story which she had used had the shape of the Virginia social history which she had been employing all through her career. I do not think that Ellen Glasgow in writing *Barren Ground* intended to make a commentary on social history or even to celebrate the landscape which she remembered and loved from her youth, but social history gives her the structure of a plot as the land and the landscape give her a massive symbolic value for depletion, exhaustion, and renewal. Her own story is the story of Dorinda, the story of triumphant fortitude and self-renunciation which leave the world in which they are exercised a better place because the exerciser has lived in it. In this sense *Barren Ground*, the most personal, private, and individual of Ellen Glasgow's novels, is, on one level, a microcosm of southern history with its plot shaped, as all her work was, by her sense of what has happened in the social history of the Commonwealth of Virginia.

Faulkner's August Avatars

For most of us William Faulkner represents the deep South as no other American novelist does. *Light in August* is the novel from Faulkner's major period which is the most readily accessible and direct a record of a southern community. It alone of the major Yoknapatawpha novels is self-contained, with its main characters independent of the major families of the county, and its actions not dependent on other works in the series for beginning, middle, or end; furthermore, its difficulties are in the interpretation of events and people rather than in surface language, as in *The Sound and the Fury,* or in decisions about the reliability of narrators, as in *Absalom, Absalom!* Hence, we might expect here a clear and direct transcript of life in a Deep South town, drawn from its author's long, personal experience. This expectation is strengthened by Faulkner's declaration at the University of Virginia, that "the writer has got to write in terms of his environment" and his remark about *Light in August*: "that story began with Lena Grove, the idea of the young girl with nothing, pregnant, determined to find her sweetheart." So that we might expect simple characters sharply presented in a clearly defined environment.

But such does not prove to be the case. "What a romance this is," Geismar unfairly says in *Writers in Crisis,* "the central love affair of Faulkner's maturity—this colored Romeo and abolitionist Juliet of Jefferson, Mississippi; the amoral mulatto and the starved spinster; the brutal criminal and the aging nymphomaniac. We come at last to the vicious conjunction in Faulkner's work of the Negro and the Female, the twin furies of Faulkner's deep southern Waste Land; but a waste land, quite unlike Eliot's, of demons and incubae rather than pallid clerks, one which

129

is built on diseased fury and ends, indeed, not with a whimper but a bang."

If a traditional realist such as Trollope or George Eliot or Howells or even John O'Hara had decided to portray Oxford, Mississippi, he would have been working in a tradition in which the novelist attempted to become a subtle and profound recorder of contemporary life; and Yoknapatawpha County might have become another Barset or Middlemarch or Gibbsville, rich with the texture of common life, filled with Lionel Trilling's "hum and buzz of implication," a place of the ordinary, the untroubled, the commonplace. Its record would be essentially that of its controlling middle class and their ideas, ideals, and attitudes, an account of how they act out their public roles in a system of social conventions and tribal rituals.

Of course, counties like Yoknapatawpha do have ordered societies, businesses, governments, their own hum and buzz of implication, their ruling families as well as the poor, the criminals, the defeated, the sharecroppers, and the white trash of whom Faulkner often wrote. Some southern writers, and very good ones too, have been primarily interested in that social world, and have worked with diligence and integrity to portray it—certainly Ellen Glasgow did, and so did T.S. Stribling (from whom, on occasion, Faulkner borrowed). But Faulkner's intent is clearly neither to portray that social world nor to use the tools of the realistic novelist in writing the chronicle of his county.

None of us, I trust, is naïve enough to believe there is a single South or one proper way to write about it. The Southern Piedmont can be the subject matter through which Thomas Wolfe explores and defines his own inner being, so that his southern experience and his southern rhetoric become the instruments of intense self-expression. Kentucky and its history, Louisiana and its politics can be the subjects for Robert Penn Warren's philosophical novels, in which man's need to come to terms with a badly flawed world are explored. South Georgia can be the material for Flannery O'Connor's chilling parables of man's insatiable hunger for salvation. Upper Georgia and South Carolina are the matters from which Erskine Caldwell can fashion his inquiries into the sociological implications of poverty and deprivation. Louisiana is a sufficient subject for Walker Percy's explorations of the existential malaise of our century. Virginia was an adequate subject matter for Ellen Glasgow's fictional portrayals of social history. Each of these writers use the materials of some portion of the South to communicate their visions of reality. And in the works of most of them, the South portrayed is more readily recognized than it is in Faulkner.

Yet Faulkner's work is firmly grounded in the places, the people, the events, and the history of the Deep South. The small-town Deep South is his primary subject matter. At the University of Virginia, he said, when asked about his use of Christian materials in *Light in August, Requiem for a Nun*, and *A Fable*: "Remember, the writer must write out of his background. He must write out of what he knows and the Christian legend is part of any Christian's background, especially the background of a country boy, a southern country boy. My life was passed, my childhood, in a very small Mississippi town, and that was part of my background. I grew up with that. I assimilated that, took that in without even knowing it. It's just there." Elsewhere he referred to the materials of his fiction as the lumber a carpenter uses to build something or as the tools available to him for making something. Quite clearly, the basic lumber supply for William Faulkner was the southern small-town world in which he grew up. But in these comments Faulkner always subordinates the material that he gets from "the lumber room" of his memory and experience to "what he is trying to tell." Thus, if these remarks are taken seriously, the faithful reproduction of life in a southern small town is not one of his intentions and never was. Almost everyone reading Faulkner's works has sensed that he is not describing the South but using it for other purposes than simply its description or definition.

Regina K. Fadiman, after a study of the various manuscripts, reconstructs the process by which *Light in August* came into being and the changes which apparently occurred in Faulkner's intention for the book. The first version was concerned with the forward-moving narrative laid in the present. It began with the present second chapter, thus showing the centrality that Gail Hightower had for Faulkner in his initial concept of the story. In this first form the novel was a Gothic account of the effect of a brutal murder on a community and in particular its effect on Lena Grove, Gail Hightower, and Byron Bunch, what Mrs. Fadiman calls "the anatomy of the society of which these bystanders are a part." At the next stage Faulkner made his first major change in the direction of the story by the insertion of what are now chapters six through twelve, Joe Christmas's memories of his earlier life, told through his emotions and attitudes. In this long flashback Christmas's role underwent significant elaboration. Where, in the first draft, Faulkner had said with the authority of the omniscient author that Christmas had Negro blood, he now established that forever-to-be-unanswered question of whether he does or not and thus makes Joe's problem, in part at least, his uncertainty as to what he is racially in a community of marked racial polarities. In this new section, he adds most, although not all, the details in Joe Christmas's life which closely parallel those in the life of Christ, and makes the positive statement that Christmas died on Friday at the age of thirty-three. In later revisions Faulkner changed the day of Joe's death and so modified the dating of the story and the age of Joe Christmas that it is now impossible to determine what age Joe was at the time of his death, there being within the book evidence for at least three different ages. The ambiguities about dates and ages in the novel are real, and they come, at least in part, out of Faulkner's desire to modify the emphasis he had originally placed upon Christmas's having died at the age of thirty-three on Friday. After the extensive revising, rearranging, and shifting of chapters that the manuscript versions underwent, Faulkner arrived finally at the structure in which the story opens with Lena Grove's entering Jefferson and closes with Lena Grove and Byron Bunch on the furniture dealer's wagon. In the revisions of this material, too, the Biblical allusions are lessened. Originally the furniture dealer of the last chapter had been a cattle dealer. In the first version it was not

used furniture but cattle in his truck. Thus the parallels between Lena, Bunch, the baby, and the cattle to the Holy Family were far more pronounced than they are in the final version
of the novel. The last significant change in the story was the addition in chapter 1 of the reference to Keats's "Ode on a Grecian
Urn," in which Lena is described "like something moving forever and without progress across an urn." The late addition of
this urn image, the first of many which appear in the novel, in-
dicates Faulkner's intention to have Lena represent a positive,
optimistic, healthy, and serene contrast to the hatred of everything female that is one of the two motivating forces for Joe
Christmas's destructive actions.

The aspect of the central events of *Light in August* on which
Faulkner wished to place his greatest emphasis and from which
he wished to extract the profoundest meaning of the novel is a
function, in major part, of contrast and counterpoint among
the elements of the book, of the order in which actions take
place, and of the nature of his imagery and of his direct and indirect allusions. These are methods of investing narrative with
meaning used by many contemporary novelists, but they are
not the methods by which a novelist usually tries to reproduce
realistically the nature and quality of life in a small town. One
of the most obvious characteristics of modernism is that it no
longer finds in the literal reproduction of actuality, in the system of social mimesis that was a motive impulse for realistic fiction, an adequate means of representation. The modernist
agrees with Dostoevski, when in his search for what he called
"the inmost essence of truth," he says, "Arid observations of everyday trivialities I have long ceased to regard as realism. . . .
How paltry and petty is such a way of driving home actualities!
. . . I have a totally different conception of truth and realism
from that of our 'realists'." As William Barrett has asserted,
"The imagination [of the Modern novelist] has had to free itself
from the tedium of reportage. Much destruction has ensued on
the way. . . . but in this rage to destroy may be present the
birthpangs of a new reality struggling for expression." Not finding in nature itself an adequate subject for the expression of

artistic intention the modernist novelist uses it as the raw materials out of which, through method of presentation, distortion, and rearrangement, he creates meanings individual to himself. This method Faulkner used from the beginning of his career. As James Burnham pointed out in 1931, "Faulkner is using the data of observation only as a material in the construction of his own world. It is to be judged not as imitation but as creation, by the emotional integrity with which it is formed."

François Pitavy has accurately observed, in his superb study *Faulkner's Light in August*, that "impressionism is realism pushed to extremes, a desire to imitate the inimitable and to capture evanescence, like the Seine at Les Andelys or Reims Cathedral swathed in a unique and insubstantial veil of mist. Expressionism, on the other hand, seeks not to fix the quality of a given instant, not to make 'a moment's monument' but to reconstruct from the artist's own reactions and the elements of his vision, a coherent reality which does not show fleeting appearances but the essential qualities, as he has glimpsed them beyond and through these appearances. The results may appear disturbingly idiosyncratic insofar as the work is the outcome of an inner compulsion working with elements which may well have been distorted in passing through the prism of a personality." It is this kind of modernist expressionism which is dominant in Faulkner's work and is his primary mode in *Light in August*. In converting the materials of his direct experience into expressionistic statements of inner and often abstract thoughts and feelings, Faulkner removes the world of *Light in August* from any close direct correspondence to Oxford in Lafayette County, Mississippi.

In giving special meaning and depth to his picture of these denizens of Jefferson, Faulkner has freely borrowed from a great variety of mythic sources and particularly from the Bible. As Michael Millgate, and others, have asserted, it is possible to see parallels between characters and actions in the novel and the world's mythology, particularly as it is described in *The Golden Bough*. Parallels exist not only between Joe Christmas and Christ but also between Joe and Oedipus. The richness of such allusion and parallel is certainly real. On the other hand, such matters should be pursued with some restraint, for, as Malcolm Cowley has pointed out, Faulkner was not a deeply educated man, knew little Greek, and was probably dependent on *The Golden Bough* for most of his mythic parallels.

There is, however, no question of his deep immersion in and thorough knowledge of the materials of the Bible and the events in the life of Christ. I shall not here attempt to enumerate the many parallels that exist in the novel between its events and the Christ story. They are, I believe, obvious to any reader familiar with the New Testament. There has been a tendency on the part of most critics approaching *Light in August* to see such parallels as Joe Christmas's being found on Christmas Day, being the child of an unwed mother, having the initials "JC," and the paralleling of the events of Holy Week during the last week of his life as something to be explained away because of the brutal nature of Joe Christmas's life and the quality and seeming nihilism of his suffering and death. This, however, is, I think, a fairly naïve reaction. The use of the Christ story in twentieth-century literature for the purposes of enriching and deepening meaning is very widespread, and in most cases, as Theodore Ziolkowski has pointed out in *The Fictional Transfigurations of Jesus*, the twentieth-century user of the story of Jesus is much more likely to portray the "suffering servant" aspect of Christ's story than the aspect of the Redeemer. Faulkner, in using the aspect of Christ most vividly described in the Book of Isaiah, chapter 53, was following a tradition widespread in Europe and often present in America. In any event, the extensive reference to the mythologies of various religions and the specific parallels to the Christian religion all serve to elevate, to deepen, to make more mysterious and more important the characters whose actions make up the structure of *Light in August*.

Pitavy points out how often adjectives are used in sylleptic constructions, such as "anonymous and deliberate wagons," "a spent and satiate beach," "bright and hurried garments." Oxymoron is also a frequent device, as in "motionless wheels rising," "woods at once static and fluid," "deliberate random," "gaunt and flabby." Words are run together, and punctuation is often omitted. All of these devices force language out of its simple denotative functions and invest it with special connotative and rhetorical qualities. Clearly Faulkner values the mimetic aspects of language less than nonimitative qualities. An abstractness, a play with ideas, is involved in such linguistic uses —and play with ideas only vaguely related to the literal qualities of what is being ostensibly described.

Furthermore, characters are not portrayed richly or realistically, but are sketched in outline, often in terms of dominant traits, such as Lena Grove's serenity or Joe Christmas's shadow. These traits or tags are frequently nonphysical, not what can be seen about a character physically but what is sensed about a character intellectually or emotionally. The attitude of the character telling the narrative or the attitude of the persona producing the book—that is, the emotional reaction rather than a literal description of what is seen—determines the qualities assigned to the actors. The people of the book are described basically in terms of qualities rather than physical attributes, in outlines rather than fully fleshed figures. What we see of Lena is her distended stomach, her men's shoes, her dress, the dust she walks in. I defy a reader to tell me how Faulkner says she looks. The landscape, too, is described in terms of sharp contrast and severely marked outlines—blacks and whites, lights and darks, moonlight, sharply etched outlines, the blackness of pits, the brightness of day. A landscape described by such means becomes also a projection of an emotional attitude toward the characters and events within that landscape. Here too accuracy is surrendered to abstractness and expressionism.

The story itself has crucial ambiguous situations—not the open-ended and unresolved outcome of actions typical of the realistic novel but fundamental confusions about the basic facts of the story. Does Joe Christmas have Negro blood? No one really knows. Whether it is credible or not, Lena Grove becomes bewildered about the identity of her child and begins to confuse it with Joe Christmas, whom she has never seen. How old Joe is is a needlessly vexed critical problem, for it cannot be

solved. There are many more such fundamental matters of uncertainty, the primary object of which seems to be to enrich the
possibilities of meaning and suggestion in the story. In contrast,
in Henry James' *The Ambassadors* the identity of the "vulgar
household article" being manufactured at Woollett is never disclosed, but this does not create ambiguity, for the fact that it is
never disclosed is a significant piece of data about the characters and serves a direct and clarifying purpose. The uncertain-
ties in *Light in August*, on the other hand, are much more like
those in *The Scarlet Letter*, where the multiplicity of judgments, with no evidence to support any single one as the correct
one, serves the purpose not of clarifying aspects of the book but
of enormously increasing the possible symbolic values of the
book. Faulkner seems to use factual ambiguity in *Light in August* as an intensifying and enriching device much as Hawthorne did.

Light in August has three largely separate story strands.
These strands are the story of Joe Christmas, his murder of Joanna Burden, a retrospect of his earlier life, and his death; the
story of Gail Hightower and his re-introduction into life through
Lena Grove and Joe Christmas and a retrospect of his marriage
and ministry; and the story of Lena Grove, her search for the
father of her child, its birth, and Byron Bunch's love for her.

Faulkner presents these three essentially distinct stories with
only loose plot links among them and with their themes sharply
juxtaposed. Yet within each strand Faulkner so uses language
that there is formed an intense emotional and introspective involvement of the reader with the characters of that strand. This
method makes the characters in *Light in August* intense, unre-
alistic, and larger than life. To discover the meaning of *Light in
August*, the novel must be read in such a way that the mind and
feelings of the reader are subordinated to the emotions of the
characters as they are expressionistically represented in the
three strands of the story. Then these emotions and feelings
must be held in the mind in a sufficiently firm suspension that,
when the book has been completed, the reader can go back in
memory and reassess these emotional responses and expression-

istic statements in each of the three major narrative strands. By this reassessment he can find a meaning being suggested not by any single character or story strand but through the counter-pointing of all of them. The counterpointing is quite as challenging to the reader as the reconstruction of complex narrative in *Absalom, Absalom!* or the penetration of stream-of-consciousness metaphors and syntactical disjunctions in *The Sound and the Fury,* and it is more likely to be misread than either of those challenging novels because, on the surface, it seems simpler and more direct. In a sense the major juxtaposition is that of alienation in the story of Joe Christmas and Joanna Burden and that of acceptance in the stories of Lena Grove, Byron Bunch, and Gail Hightower. In this respect *Light in August* seems both thematically and structurally like Melville's *Moby-Dick,* which Faulkner declared that he re-read every year. Joe Christmas defies an alien universe, as Ahab does, and Gail Hightower learns acceptance, as Ishmael does, and in each case one must survey the total novel to see where the author stands.

The result of these complex methods of storytelling and this presentation of characters in terms of essences rather than traits is that Yoknapatawpha County and its county seat, Jefferson, a small agricultural bit of land inhabited by small farmers, merchants, lawyers, artisans, tenant farmers, and blacks is elevated to an almost cosmic level. "The larger than life figures of Joe Christmas and his grandfather, and Joanna Burden and her family, stand as epic representations of the racist South of actuality, cursed by its own guilt," as R.G. Collins has said. This burden is a heavy one to be borne by people as simple, weak, and unimportant as the actual persons of the novel. If the story of Joe Christmas is, as Faulkner himself called it, a tragedy, then Joe Christmas, an itinerant sawmill worker, is made to play a role earth-shaking in its magnitude. In terms of importance, he must take his place with kings and makers, with rulers and shakers; for the tragic protagonist must loom larger than life, while in a literal way Joe Christmas is smaller than the common middle-class life which is the normal subject of realistic fiction. But Faulkner's figures give the impression of being vast earth-towering figures, outlined against vast, luridly colored skies, drawn larger than life, with feelings that are of cosmic importance. They shape the nature of the universe by the steps they take and the choices they make.

In one sense these characters loom as vast phantasmagorical shapes, for the reason that Mr. Compson gives Quentin at one time in *Absalom, Absalom!* when he says that the people in the Sutpen story were "people too as we are, and victims too as we are, but victims of a different circumstance, simpler and therefore, integer for integer, larger, more heroic and the figures therefore more heroic too." Certainly this process of simplification and reduction works to invest these characters with special significance. Cleanth Brooks sees the controlling frame of *Light in August* as pastoral, in the sense that the large issues with which the book deals are examined in simpler and less complex circumstances than those of the great world. Certainly the Lena Grove story has some elements of the pastoral in it, but in a major sense these elements exist as pastoral, it seems to me, primarily in contrast to the Gothic violence of the Joe Christmas story and, in part at least, because of the references to John Keats's Grecian Urn. Also Faulkner's habit of giving his characters descriptive names—Christmas, Burden, Bunch, Hightower, Grove—gives them a degree of unearthliness. They become, as Faulkner insists by repeatedly applying the term *avatar* to them, manifestations or embodiments of concepts, philosophies, or traditions. All this is, indeed, a form of highly romantic art, but also an art that partakes of modernism.

Since the ultimate meaning of *Light in August* is a function of the way its readers put together the counterpointed pieces of the book and the degree to which they recognize the unreliability of the narration and the expressionistic nature of the writing, it has received a great variety of interpretations. It has been read as a romantic, Gothic horror story, the tale of an atrocious crime marked by perverse sex and great violence and told in lurid episodes in a book of unrelieved darkness. Certainly the materials for such an interpretation are present, though the extent to which Faulkner fails to play out on stage the major scenes in such a Gothic murder story should cause the reader some hesitation before he accepts it. Faulkner himself tended to talk about the novel in terms of its separate elements, describing the tragedy of a man who could not find an identity and the story of Lena Grove as a story celebrating the strength and beauty of womanhood. On one occasion I became strongly impressed with the very large number of parallels to Christ in the book and described it as an assertion of the need eternally to replicate Christ's act of expiation in a world of guilt. Others have seen it as primarily a comment on the intolerable situation of the Negro race in the South. Irene Edmonds saw it and condemned it as Faulkner's attempt to utilize the theme of the tragic mulatto. Carl Benson described it as the tragedy of isolation. Cleanth Brooks sees it as the study of separation from community. To a certain degree, all of these readings are correct, but none is correct if it is to be regarded as exclusively true.

But whatever meaning we see embodied in these huge figures who loom before us brilliantly conceived in outline form, defined in expressionistic language, and performing cosmic actions, one level of meaning which they embody is still clearly related to the South in which William Faulkner grew up, the problems which that South confronts—particularly the problems which grow out of the existence in it of two different races and a widespread concept of racial superiority—and the shape of its history. In order to look at this meaning of *Light in August* in regard to the rest of the story, I think it would be helpful to attempt to make the distinction between *symbolism*, such as that of the black pit, the cracked urn, Joe Christmas's shadow, and other recurrent images so used that they suggest abstract meanings independent of and transcendent to the literal level of the story and *representation*, the way by which characters and actions stand for the class of things of which they are themselves literally a part. Malcolm Cowley recently made this distinction with regard to *The Sound and the Fury* when he said,

"Its principal theme is the decline of the Compson family, which stands by synecdoche (not symbolism) for the Old South."

In this sense the characters of *Light in August* are very closely related to the history and the social problems of the South, though they are not very accurate or realistic and certainly not mimetic portrayals of the people of that South. If they are avatars, they are such as representations or embodiments of aspects of the South, its people, and its history, as well as manifestations of cosmic Truths. The South of *Light in August* is essentially the white man's South, and the role of the black man in the South is that role as viewed by the white. Hence the tragedy of Joe Christmas, a tragedy which grows from his uncertainty about whether he has black blood or not, is not an attempt to represent the position of the black man in southern society but rather to intensify to the utmost degree the effect of the myth of racial discrimination and racial superiority upon the white man. Joe is an avatar, not of the black southerner but of the racist white southerner. For this reason in the successive revisions of the book the original certainty that Faulkner had about Joe Christmas's possessing Negro blood becomes increasingly uncertain. So far as the society in which he lives is concerned, as Collins has pointed out, Joe "is just another white on the level of reality; his alienation is imposed by himself, by his own racial prejudices against himself." The horror with which Joe Christmas views the possibility of his having Negro blood is not a black man's horror but a white man's, and the problem of identity is not the black man's problem but the white man's. In Joe's case, we start, as Faulkner did, with the question of Joe Christmas's paternity as a question of race; but very quickly it becomes not a question of race but a synecdochic view of the myth of inferior races, and finally it becomes simply a symbol of man's inevitable guilt, a guilt which must be expiated. If Joe Christmas is intended in some way to be a Christ figure and his death is intended in some way to be a crucifixion, it was necessary for theological reasons that he finally have no Negro blood, since Negro blood serves for him as a sin of the father transmitted to the children, a form of original sin, inescapable,

141

out of the past, borne in the present without personal guilt. Thus Joe Christmas in dying needs to die for a guilt which is not his own and which he assumes for the community. In the magnificent passage describing the death and castration of Joe Christmas, in which his black blood ascends toward heaven, Faulkner assigns him this role of communal expiation.

In the same way Lena Grove, who is first an unfortunate hillbilly Juliet, becomes a classical figure of the indomitable force of woman so that she moves through the book with the serene assurance and optimistic force of the unthinking but forever prevailing forward movement of life. She is an avatar of the southern woman who prevails and triumphs. Byron Bunch, a simple Romeo in a small-town love story, becomes an avatar of the common people and the forces for good, for the continuation of life and justice which these common people represent. Gail Hightower, a failed and irresponsible minister, becomes in a sense a type of all the inheritors of the noble southern tradition of honor and chivalry who are lost now in its distorted memory and in its destructive worship. This avatar must somehow be awakened by the forces of life, the goodness of the common people, and the common guilt of man to his responsibilities in the world that he inhabits. Joanna Burden, the southern daughter of an abolitionist, committed now to an abstract liberalism regarding race and racial problems, becomes an avatar of the southern liberal whose approach to the racial problem is itself degrading to the person whose salvation she attempts to secure. Each of these major characters, thus, becomes representative of a segment of society and an aspect of southern history.

Through this process a tale of brutal murder becomes an assertion of life and of the prevailing of the good common people, and it issues a call to those who have inherited a noble tradition to awaken to their responsibilities and recognize their duties. And thus the novelist has transmuted the materials of a southern Gothic romance into a statement about man and the cosmos —a teleologically oriented statement of ultimate truths. Like the prophet Isaiah, whose apocalyptic warnings and admonitions he echoes, Faulkner starts out to describe the sad state of a society and ends up describing the ultimate hope of man. Thus he uses the methods of modernism to shape his fable of the troubled South into a prophetic instrument whose ultimate theme, like all great art, is as old as time.

The Dwarf on Wolfe's Shoulder

In a letter to Ernest Hemingway, Maxwell Perkins wrote, "I told Tom [Wolfe] that a whole lot of fine stuff he had in simply ought to come out because it resulted in blurring a very important effect. Literally, we sat here for an hour thereafter without saying a word, while Tom glowered and pondered and fidgeted in his chair. Then he said, 'Well, then will you take the responsibility?' And I said, 'I simply got to take the responsibility. And what's more,' I said, 'I will be blamed, either way.'"[1] That brief statement summarizes the most famous—or perhaps the word should be "notorious"—editor-author relationship in the history of American writing—that of Thomas Wolfe and Maxwell Perkins, editor of Charles Scribner's Sons, Publishers, and it defines clearly Perkins's responsibility.

This relationship has been used repeatedly to condemn Wolfe's work as formless, uncontrolled, the spontaneous overflow of overly impassioned feeling that had to be subjected to the logic and rigor of an intelligent editorial blue pencil before it could find the light of day. From Bernard DeVoto's famous charge in the *Saturday Review of Literature* that "Genius Is Not Enough" and that novels cannot be produced by "the assembly line at Scribners"[2] to Sharon Doten's note in the *Papers of the Bibliographical Society of America* in 1974 taking me seriously to task for asserting that in the short novels Wolfe displays a sense of form absent from his huge rambling novels,[3] critics have, with a few exceptions, seen the instrumental hand of Maxwell Perkins as one essential to the shaping of the outpourings of Wolfe's untrammeled genius into publishable words. For example, Norman Friedman in his recent *Form and Meaning in Fiction*, almost casually says: "As Thomas Wolfe

144

wrote to Fitzgerald, there are great putter-inners as well as great taker-outers, but Wolfe's own practice as a great putter-inner . . . is not always successful—other great putter-inners, after all, did not need a Maxwell Perkins to boil down their manuscripts into publishable shape."[4]

The facts in the case are relatively simple. In 1928 Madeleine Boyd, acting as agent for Wolfe, submitted the manuscript of what was to become *Look Homeward, Angel* to Maxwell Perkins, after it had been declined by Boni and Liveright, Harcourt Brace, Longmans, Green and Company, and Covici-Friede. Perkins was impressed with the manuscript, believed that it could be made into "a form publishable by us," and worked with Wolfe to give it publishable form. He had Wolfe remove a few episodes, shift Gant's long trip to California from Part II to Part I, delete a large block of material at the beginning of the novel—perhaps 70,000 words—dealing with W.O. Gant's earlier life, and cut some of Wolfe's digressions on politics, morals, and religion, and some of the life histories of minor characters.[5] But in actual fact, *Look Homeward, Angel*, when it appeared in 1929, was as close to the author's own work as the published forms of the first novels of exuberant writers usually are. There is no question that the idea of the book, the language of the book, the episodes of the book, and the shape of the book are Thomas Wolfe's and not Maxwell Perkins's, or that of Wolfe's four novels, it, and it alone, represents his clearly realized authorial intention.

With the struggle to produce his next book Wolfe's relationships to Maxwell Perkins became elaborate and intense, and Perkins's role became major. Between 1930 and 1934, Wolfe was deeply involved in a powerful struggle to produce his next work.[6] The struggle finally evolved into a situation where, as Perkins expressed it, "We work every evening from 8:30 (or as near as Tom can come to it) until 10:30 or 11:00, and Tom does actual writing at times, and does it well, where pieces have to be joined up. We are organizing the book. That is the best part of the work we are doing. It will be pretty well integrated in the end, and vastly more effectively arranged."[7] Out of this effort emerged *Of Time and the River*, which Perkins sent to the press in September, 1934, while Wolfe was at the Chicago World's Fair, and which was changed from first person to third person by editors in the Scribner's editorial offices.

That Wolfe was unhappy with the result of this editorial collaboration he made painfully clear in his correspondence about the book. In a letter to Perkins in March, 1935, after seeing his first copy of the book, he wrote, ". . . as I told you many times, I did not care whether the final length of the book was 300, 500, or a 1000 pages, so long as I had realized completely and finally my full intention—and that was not realized. I still sweat with anguish—with a sense of irremediable loss—at the thought of what another six months would have done to that book. . . ."[8] Perkins had known well before publication that Wolfe did not approve of what had been done to the book. In January, 1935, when he learned that the book was being dedicated to him, he wrote, ". . . you cannot, and should not, try to change your conviction that I have deformed your book, or at least prevented it from coming to perfection. It is therefore impossible for you sincerely to dedicate it to me, and it ought not to be done. . . . what I have done has destroyed *your* belief in it [*Of Time and the River*] and you must not act inconsistently with that fact."[9] Many factors entered into this discontent, and they were exacerbated by a series of events and libel suits which occurred between the publication of *Of Time and the River* and Wolfe's final break with Scribner's in the late fall of 1937 when he signed a contract with Edward Aswell for the future publication of his work by Harper and Brothers. Among the reasons Wolfe stated were Perkins's unwillingness to allow him to express fully what he believed to be his Marxian sentiments, Perkins's unwillingness to allow him to write of Charles Scribner's Sons in books which Scribner's was going to publish, Perkins's unwillingness to allow him to publish in the order that he chose, and, in general, Perkins's control of the nature and shape of his work.[10] But behind it all there lingers the sense of frustration and angry bitterness expressed in Wolfe's long, long letter in the spring of 1935, when he read his first copy of *Of*

Time and the River and declared that he could have made it a better book if he had had the chance to do so.[11] Thus ended an editor-author relationship but without ending the strong personal feeling of deep affection and friendship between the two men, a feeling which resulted in Wolfe's last written words being a letter to Perkins and in Perkins's being appointed literary executor for the Wolfe estate.

At his death in 1938, Wolfe left a great mass of manuscript out of which Edward Aswell quarried two large novels, *The Web and the Rock* and *You Can't Go Home Again*, and a collection of short fiction and fragments, *The Hills Beyond*. Aswell was the major and shaping influence on the posthumous books, but Wolfe's personal relationship with him extended only from the 1937 Christmas season until his departure for the West in the early summer of 1938. Aswell's editorial task was to create—not really too strong a word—two novels out of a mass of incomplete materials following Wolfe's outline, and to do it without access to the author for revision or change. Aswell was interviewed about the condition of this material by Richard S. Kennedy, when Kennedy was working on his *The Window of Memory*. Kennedy's notes on this interview are illuminating. They read "Aswell didn't know where to start. Book written at various times, main character had several different names. . . . He followed Outline where he could, but many links were yet unwritten, e.g. about bank's failure in his home town, etc. Aswell supplied a few links, picked up what materials he thought would fit in, etc. finally the books published."[12] Thus the great question of publishers' effect on Wolfe's writing is primarily a question of the influence upon his work of Maxwell Perkins.

When Thomas Wolfe stormed the citadels of the great cities, he was indeed the traditional young man from the provinces, and he brought with him a sense so foreign to the role of artist in a center of culture that he had difficulty seeing himself in the role in which his great talent and his literary success cast him. He was a North Carolina mountain boy, and to an appreciable extent he never outgrew that role. He was unsure of himself, as he tells poignantly in *The Story of a Novel*: "I don't know when it occurred to me first that I would be a writer. . . . I may have thought it would be a fine thing because a writer was a man like Lord Byron or Lord Tennyson or Longfellow or Percy Bysshe Shelley. A writer was a man who was far away . . . a man from a kind of remote people. . . . We're still more perturbed by the strangeness of the writing profession than any other people I have known on earth."[13] He found it impossible to believe fully that he was a writer. "I would think," he said, "that somehow I was practising an imposture on my readers."[14]

And he found, too, in his editor Maxwell Perkins a descendant of New England Brahmins, a man of great grace, tact, urbanity, and near genius, and he was thoroughly overawed by him. At no point in Wolfe's career did he have the full courage of his artistic convictions, and certainly not when he had to pit what he took to be his ignorance against Perkins's knowledge and grace. He did his work with a kind of romantic self-expression, and the test which he applied to it was its seeming rightness to him. The ability to analyze deeply the intricate interrelationships of his work seems not to have been a part of his aesthetic or artistic equipment. Yet he had, too, an awareness of the special genius which was his. "I am," he could declare to his mother as early as 1923, "inevitable,"[15] and not only believe it but know it to be true. Hence, he had the artistic assurance that allowed him to do his work with firmness and surety, but he lacked the self-confidence to assert that it was right when it was challenged.

Andrew Turnbull reports that Maxwell Perkins once told his wife that "he would like to be a little dwarf on the shoulders of a great general, advising him what to do and what not to do without anyone's noticing."[16] As the most famous and successful literary editor of his generation, Maxwell Perkins in a sense achieved that role. Hemingway, who seems to have recognized this quality in his editor, remarked after the deaths of Wolfe and Fitzgerald, "You realize you're through, don't you? All your generals are dead."[17] And indeed these three—Hemingway, Fitzgerald, and Wolfe—were generals, the shape of whose career Maxwell Perkins saw himself as significantly shaping.

These writers had enormous talent, and Perkins built his career and a revitalized position for Charles Scribner's Sons out of what he was able to do with this talent. As early as 1918 he had seen in the first version of Fitzgerald's *This Side of Paradise* a great new talent, and when in 1920 a revised and improved version of that book was published by Scribner's, it proved Fitzgerald to be the spokesman of the younger generation, and the book became what Turnbull has called "the first rolling stone in a literary landslide for Scribner's."[18] Following Fitzgerald's advice Perkins solicited the manuscript of Hemingway's *The Sun Also Rises* and worked heroically to see that the book was published. In 1929 he detected in the sprawling manuscript "O Lost" the talent which would make a great career for Wolfe. In each case Perkins had been a formative influence in the launching of a major career. And to these five-star generals he added the lesser but still impressive work of majors and colonels: the short stories of Ring Lardner, the works of the ex-cowboy Will James, the historical novels of James Boyd, Willard Huntington Wright's astoundingly successful Philo Vance detective stories published under the pseudonym of S.S. Van Dine, the regional works of Marjorie Kinnan Rawlings, and the early work of James Jones. All of these writers to some degree benefited significantly from Perkins's editorial judgment and guidance. His criticism, he felt, was offered tentatively, obliquely, half reluctantly. Turnbull quotes one writer who said that asking Perkins for advice was like dropping pebbles down a well and listening for the splash. "Don't *ever* defer to my judgment" he told Fitzgerald.[19] And certainly his numerous protests that he did not write Wolfe's book have the ring of baffled sincerity about them.

Yet almost certainly Maxwell Perkins did not understand Thomas Wolfe, however well he knew and however much he loved him. To imagine Perkins or anyone else persuading Hemingway to do anything contrary to Hemingway's own sense of artistic propriety is almost ridiculous. Perkins once said, "Nobody ever edited Hemingway, beyond excising a line or two,"[20] and much the same was true for Fitzgerald. There seems every reason to believe that Perkins made few distinctions in regard to this quality in his "three generals." The suggestions he made to Wolfe for deletions, changes, or modifications in Wolfe's manuscripts initially resulted in explosions that were almost violent, but almost always Wolfe returned in a day or two and made the changes that Perkins had proposed. That this represented Wolfe's basic lack of confidence in his own artistic judgment rather than his having given careful consideration to the matter and having come to agree with Perkins's judgment seems never to have occurred to Perkins. The result was that Perkins continued through the crucial years of Wolfe's career to sit as the dwarf on this general's shoulder, directing the deployment of one of the massive talents which America has produced almost certainly without realizing the full extent to which that deployment represented a distortion.

At this point it is necessary to examine at least briefly the relationship of the whole and the parts in Wolfe's work. There is no question that everything Wolfe was writing through his mature career was a part of what he called "The Book," a record of one man's experience in the world, and every part of it, small or large, was a portion of what in his mind was an unbroken fabric made of the texture and quality of his own life. Unless his artistic ambitions would have changed—and there is no reason to think that they would have—were Wolfe still living today, all the parts of the work which he would have produced would share intimate relationships with all the others. For Wolfe was truly a romantic expressive artist who drew the substance of his work out of himself and his observations in the world. To say that is not, however, to suggest that Wolfe never wrote anything except as a patterned portion of a consciously shaped total work.

A comparison with Faulkner may be illuminating. With a few exceptions, the short stories, short novels, and long novels which taken together constitute the massive Yoknapatawpha legend are similar to how Wolfe worked. There is no reason to think that the history, denizens, and landscape of Yoknapatawpha County sprang full grown into Faulkner's mind in the late

1920s and that piece by piece he filled in segments of a whole that existed before the appearance of the first work in the Yoknapatawpha Saga. Instead he published novels, short stories, and short novels dealing with various portions of the history, the landscape, the people, and the experiences of that imaginary county, and when the work could at last be viewed by George O'Donnell in the late 1930s[21] or by Malcolm Cowley in the middle 1940s,[22] it could be seen that the parts fitted together to form an incomplete whole, although the separate elements which made that whole had been woven of many different strands and consisted of works in different genres. A similar kind of development occurs in Wolfe's work. Whether in brief and self-contained episodes which could be published as short stories in magazines, or in short novels of 20,000 to 40,000 words, or in novels of 600 or more pages, Wolfe's subject was the pilgrimage of a typical American through the experience of American life, and he was faithful to that subject with a consistency fully as great as that which Faulkner showed to Yoknapatawpha County.

But as portions of that experience presented themselves to his active and creative imagination, he fashioned them into units appropriate to their own length. He thought of these units as portions of a total work—"The Book"—but he wrote them in forms that made them distinct and independent of each other.[23] During his lifetime, his published works consisted of two novels, *Look Homeward, Angel* and *Of Time and the River*, *From Death to Morning*, a collection of short stories and short novels, *The Story of a Novel*, an essay in literary criticism, seven short novels, twenty-nine short stories, and two works which are not fiction and which I shall call prose poems. In addition to this, he had produced a vast body of manuscript out of which were quarried two novels, one collection of short fiction, including an incomplete novel, one short novel, and various pieces posthumously published at different times in magazines as short stories or prose poems.

At every point in Wolfe's career, his accumulated writings probably represented some such conglomeration of materials as he left Aswell to sort out. At various times he called the central figure Eugene Gant, David Hawke, John Hawke, Joe Doaks, George Webber, and other names. He wrote of him both in the third person and in the first person. Among the episodes which were to have places in the total work were materials which he was told or which he learned from others—units that were seemingly completely objective and independent, such as the short stories "In the Park," "Only the Dead Know Brooklyn," or "Child by Tiger."[24] Yet to suggest that "In the Park" is less a part of Wolfe's total experience because it deals entirely with the childhood of Esther Jack is to miss the point of Wolfe's attempt to put one man fully on record. It is, however, an example of what Perkins meant when he wrote of the stories in *From Death to Morning*, "They show how objective you can be."[25]

The issue here is very plainly one of the difference between form and material. After *Look Homeward, Angel* Wolfe seemingly was able to deal with emotions in elaborate prose poems and remembered incidents in self-contained dramatic short stories and short novels, and to depend ultimately upon some controlling frame for the places where they would finally fall in his total work. This does not mean that they needed to be fitted into some such controlling frame before they were published, and it is upon the rock of that fact that the charting of the course which Perkins made for Wolfe finally came seriously aground. In 1932 Wolfe wished to publish a fragment of the total work under the title *K-19*, an account of a long train ride to Altamont.[26] It was to have been his second book, and Perkins and Scribner's agreed with him that it would be published in this form.[27] It was actually put into production and announced, and salesmen's dummies of *K-19* were prepared and used by Scribner's salesmen. One such dummy still exists in the Thomas Wolfe Collection in the Pack Memorial Library in Asheville, North Carolina. Then Perkins decided that *K-19*—not a great work it must be admitted—should not be the one with which Wolfe would follow the great critical success of *Look Homeward, Angel*—it was not a tremendous success in the marketplace, selling only 12,000 copies during its first year. When Wolfe was making the fatal break with Perkins in 1937, this matter came very forcefully to Perkins's mind, and in his letter in response to Wolfe's twenty-eight-page diatribe, he said, "And as for publishing what you like, or being prevented from it, apart from the limitations of space, you have not been, intentionally. Are you thinking of '*K-19*'? We would have published it if you had said to do it. At the time, I said to Jack [Wheelock]: 'Maybe it's the way Tom is. Maybe we should just publish him as he comes and in the end it will be all right.'"[28] Perkins once planned to issue the short novel *No Door* in book form in 1933, but later decided against it.[29] The next work which Wolfe wished to publish was a collection of his short novels which would have included *A Portrait of Bascom Hawke, The Web of Earth,* and one other short novel.[30] Had this volume been published, it would have been, like *K-19* and *No Door,* a brief work. It would have made the publication of the Bascom Pentland material in *Of Time and the River* impossible, and it would have presented to the public a different Wolfe, one working in brief and reasonably self-contained units of the sort which he had regularly published. This work, too, was originally agreed to by Perkins and then withdrawn.

Imagine that Wolfe's career after 1929 had included *K-19* in 1932, *No Door* in 1933, and *Bascom Hawke* and *The Web of Earth* in 1934, probably the projected Hudson River people book in 1935, and then *The Good Child,* dealing with Esther Jack's life, in 1936. These would have been relatively short books, more self-controlled and objective than *Of Time and the River,* and would have reflected the way in which Wolfe normally thought and wrote. Had this happened, the expectations which were gallingly present and pressing in upon him with spiritually destructive force in *The Story of a Novel* would not have been there.[31] The image of the vastly prolific writer who lacks a sense of form or control would hardly have appeared, and the shape of his career would have been radically different. It would have been that of a man whose work is of a piece but which appears in various parts at different times with no necessary chronology to the order of its presentation nor consistency in the generic form in which it appears.

But Perkins not Wolfe made the decision, and Perkins's decision was quite different. It was that he must follow *Look Homeward, Angel* with a large book in which the materials find somehow some vast controlling organization; that they must be, not about David Hawke or John Hawke or Joe Doaks, but about Eugene Gant; that, although most of the parts had been written in the first person, they must be converted to third person in order to be consistent with *Look Homeward, Angel*;[32] and that some vast structure or controlling overarching organization must be found. Wolfe's letters during this period are a record of his endless and agonizing struggle to find such an organization, whether it be in mythology, in history, or in something else, and *Of Time and the River* is truly a cooperative effort in which the editor gives much of the large shape and the author gives the parts. The attack of Bernard DeVoto is cruel primarily because it is painfully accurate. The difficulty, however, in DeVoto's attack is that he is attacking the wrong person. He is attacking Wolfe rather than Perkins, though ultimately a basic part of talent is the ability, willingness, and tough-mindedness necessary to use it.

There can be no question of Perkins's view of Wolfe. He loved him as a man, misunderstood him as a person, found him strange, eccentric, and rather frightening, and admired his talent just this side of idolatry. He said after Wolfe's death, "He was wrestling as no artist in Europe would have to wrestle with the material of literature—a great country not yet revealed to its people. . . . It was this struggle that in a large sense governed all that he did."[33] The estimate is remarkably accurate, but Perkins seemed not to have understood that that struggle which governed all Wolfe did, did not have to determine how he did it. And it was for the best intentions in the world that Perkins, sitting as a dwarf on the shoulder of his giant, directed his struggle into the paths which he thought best and did not let that struggle take its own necessary shape.

The provincial boy from the North Carolina mountains was in this particular conflict no match for the urbane New York editor who sat on his shoulder and directed his finest talents to a vast battlefield not properly shaped for them. The results seem to me to be almost tragic, but it is a tragedy created by Wolfe's lack of artistic self-confidence.[34]

Notes

1. *Editor to Author: The Letters of Maxwell E. Perkins*, ed. John Hall Wheelock (New York, 1950), p. 91.

2. "Genius Is Not Enough," *Forays and Rebuttals*, by Bernard DeVoto (Boston, 1936); originally published in the *Saturday Review of Literature*, April 25, 1936.

3. "Thomas Wolfe's 'No Door': Some Textual Questions," *PBSA* 68 (Jan.–March, 1974), pp. 45–52. Ms. Doten argues that the version of *No Door* published in my edition of *The Short Novels of Thomas Wolfe* (New York, 1961) has no textual authority, being assembled from the versions published in magazines, a fact carefully explained in *The Short Novels*, pp. 157–58. She further argues that since there exist proposed outlines that vary substantially from the version I published that my version should have attempted to reassemble from manuscript fragments the elements listed in these outlines. There are, however, more than one outline, and Wolfe's habit of projecting vast schemas which he only partially realized is well known, as Richard S. Kennedy demonstrates repeatedly in *The Window of Memory: The Literary Career of Thomas Wolfe* (Chapel Hill, N.C., 1962). Her argument that, since Wolfe wrote *No Door* as a part of "the book," it should not be examined critically as an independent work is an argument to which this entire essay is a response in part.

4. Norman Friedman, *Form and Meaning in Fiction* (Athens, Ga., 1975), p. 100.

5. See Francis E. Skipp, "The Editing of *Look Homeward, Angel*," *PBSA* 57 (Jan.–March, 1963), 1–13; Pocket Notebook 10, March 21, 1929, to June, 1929; *The Notebooks of Thomas Wolfe*, ed. Richard S. Kennedy and Paschal Reeves (Chapel Hill, N.C., 1970), Vol. I, 316–48; Kennedy, *Window of Memory*, 173–79; Andrew Turnbull, *Thomas Wolfe* (New York, 1967), 138–45.

6. See Thomas Wolfe, *The Story of a Novel* (New York, 1936); *The Letters of Thomas Wolfe*, ed. Elizabeth Nowell (New York, 1956),

pp. 214–451 passim; Kennedy, *Window of Memory*, pp. 199–275; Turnbull, *Wolfe*, 154–206.

7. *Editor to Author*, p. 90–91.

8. *Letters*, pp. 444–45.

9. *Editor to Author*, p. 99.

10. See Wolfe's long letter of Dec. 15, 1936, to Perkins in *Letters*, pp. 575–96; and Perkins's reply of Jan. 16, 1937, in *Editor to Author*, pp. 121–26.

11. *Letters*, pp. 436–50.

12. Richard S. Kennedy, "Thomas Wolfe's Last Manuscript," *Harvard Library Bulletin* 23 (April, 1975), 209.

13. *Story of a Novel*, p. 3.

14. Ibid., p. 15.

15. *The Letters of Thomas Wolfe to His Mother*, ed. C. Hugh Holman and Sue F. Ross (Chapel Hill, N.C., 1968), p. 42.

16. Turnbull, *Wolfe*, pp. 131–32.

17. Andrew Turnbull, "Speaking of Books: Perkins' Three Generals," *New York Times Book Review*, July 16, 1967, p. 2.

18. Turnbull, *Wolfe*, p. 133. Turnbull's highly sympathetic sketch of Perkins, in *Wolfe*, pp. 127–38, is, along with Malcolm Cowley's "Profile" of Perkins, *New Yorker* (April 1, 1944), 28–36; (April 8), 30–40, the best treatment of Perkins.

19. Turnbull, *Wolfe*, 135.

20. *Editor to Author*, p. 228.

21. George Mason O'Donnell, "Faulkner's Mythology," *Kenyon Review* I (Summer, 1939), 285–99.

22. *The Portable Faulkner*, ed. Malcolm Cowley (New York, 1946). See also Malcolm Cowley, *The Faulkner-Cowley File: Letters and Memories, 1944–1962* (New York, 1966).

23. See my treatment of this aspect of Wolfe's career in "The Blest Nouvelle," in my *The Loneliness at the Core: Studies in Thomas Wolfe* (Baton Rouge, La., 1975), pp. 47–71.

24. See the essay cited above, "The Problem of Point of View," in *Loneliness at the Core*, pp. 72–85, and the Introduction to *The Thomas Wolfe Reader*, ed. C. Hugh Holman (New York, 1962).

25. *Editor to Author*, p. 104.

26. Kennedy, *Window of Memory*, pp. 247–51.

27. Turnbull, *Wolfe*, pp. 180–81.

28. *Editor to Author*, p. 123.

29. *Letters to His Mother*, p. 207; *Notebooks* II, 616.

30. *Letters to His Mother*, p. 218.

31. *Story of a Novel*, pp. 13–17.

32. Perkins, "Thomas Wolfe," *Harvard Library Bulletin*, I (Autumn, 1947), 269–77.

33. Quoted by Turnbull, in "Perkins' Three Generals," p. 27.

34. A. Scott Berg's *Max Perkins: Editor of Genius* (New York, 1978) was published after this essay was written. Although it is a very detailed account of Perkins' life, it seems to me badly to distort the Wolfe-Perkins relationship, a distortion which I discuss in "What an Editor Is," *Sewanee Review*, 86 (Fall, 1978), 572–577.

The Southern Provincial in Metropolis

One of the most common American experiences in the nineteenth and twentieth centuries has been the movement of young men of ambition and intelligence from the remote, simple, and unsophisticated places of their birth and childhood to great centers of culture, art, industry, and intellect. Such centers have been, as Theodore Dreiser once called Chicago, magnets attracting with almost irresistible force the young and ambitious who come within their orbit. New York, Boston, Philadelphia, Chicago, Los Angeles—these cities have been powerfully attractive for the eager and hopeful. Such a movement has naturally been the subject of fiction, particularly when it has an autobiographical element.

To describe this movement is to follow a tradition which has been strong in French, English, and American writing and which Lionel Trilling called the story of the Young Man from the Provinces. It is the story of Julien Sorel, which Stendhal tells in *The Red and the Black*. It is the story of Eugène Rastignac, which Balzac tells in *Père Goriot* and other of his novels in *La comédie humaine*, and the story of Lucien Chardon, which he tells in his trilogy *Lost Illusions*. It is the story of Pip, which Dickens tells in *Great Expectations*. It is the story which Gustave Flaubert tells in *Sentimental Education*. It is the story of Jay Gatsby, which Scott Fitzgerald tells in *The Great Gatsby*, and it is, with certain changes which Mr. Trilling notes, the story of Hyacinth Robinson which Henry James tells in *The Princess Casamassima*.

This Young Man from the Provinces, born and raised in simple, often rural settings, is a person of intelligence, sensitivity, high hopes, and strong ambition, but he lacks a knowledge of the ways of the world. He approaches life with directness, simplicity, and pride, and he makes great demands upon life. He is overwhelmed with wonder at its greatness and its complexities, and he sets out to seek his fortune by moving toward a metropolis. Once there he usually moves from a very obscure and poverty-stricken position to a position of some importance. In the city he is confronted with situations which he does not understand but which seem to have for him dark meanings. He wants to know how the world is run, to understand the sources of its power, to comprehend the mechanisms of its society, to be at home among its social rituals. Usually he meets some person or persons who have a position of some power in this society and who lift him out of his obscurity and set him down in places of some importance. In the city he will realize his fate, whether it be grim like that of Julien Sorel or Jay Gatsby or whether it be glorious like that of Pip. Such a form seems to be naturally suited to the frequent American experience.

The southerner, whatever his other disjunctions with the national experience, has differed from the rest of the nation in feeling this necessary attraction only in intensity; yet he has been the provincial approaching the large city in a special and different way from the midwesterner or the upstate New Yorker. In a sense New York, Boston, Chicago, San Francisco, and Los Angeles are the cultural and spiritual capitals of the regions from which most of the American provincials have come, but these cities have until very recently by no means been spiritual capitals for the southerner. The South has been until the last few decades primarily an agricultural region of communities rather than of cities. Though it has had small cities which were commercial, transportation, and shipping centers—Richmond, Baltimore, Charleston, New Orleans, and Atlanta, where the railroads began to cross in the middle of the nineteenth century —these centers have been, in a sense, the doorways to an outer world. It can be said with a reasonable degree of accuracy that the South had within its borders no cultural and intellectual capitals of the sort that London was for Englishmen, Paris for the French, Berlin for the Germans, or Boston for the New

Englanders. When the southerner has gone to the metropolis, when he has felt the strong pull of the cultural and intellectual forces concentrated in a great city, it has been to what was in many respects to him a foreign land. This fact has had a very important effect upon southern writers.

William Gilmore Simms, the most prolific and most representative of antebellum southern men of letters, had to find in New York and Philadelphia the cultural home for his work, and the pattern of his life became established so that he spent the time from October to May at his plantation seventy miles inland from Charleston and then spent the summer months in New York making contracts for the publication of his work, reading proofs, seeing books through the press, attending concerts and plays, being for a while virtually a member of the Knickerbocker group of writers and storing up a special kind of stimulus to see him through the months when he went back home. Yet he remained quintessentially a southerner, and though the issue that sharpened the difference for him was slavery, he was always a sojourner in the city, never truly a resident. The city sharpened rather than weakened his sense of what he was as a southerner and intensified rather than diminished his awareness of his differences from his fellow Americans.

Allen Tate, in the 1920s, too, went to New York City, and there he found a wider range of intellectual experiences than he had found before he left, although Nashville and Vanderbilt University were hardly rural environments. Yet his experiences with the intelligentsia of New York City, with its magazines and publications, served not to wean him away from the southernness he felt to be his most distinctive characteristic but rather to intensify it. Stark Young of Mississippi spent much of his mature life as a New York drama critic for the *New Republic*, but while he was seeing plays and criticizing them for a liberal and very urban weekly, he was also reconstructing the beautiful and ordered Old South of his imagination which is the subject of *So Red the Rose* and his other novels. Richard Wright, a Negro from the Deep South, found himself first in Chicago, then New York, and finally Paris. He never came back home again, but essentially it was the experience of being southern and black which proved to be one of the most effective subjects of his work. Hamilton Basso traveled from Louisiana to New York, from the New Orleans *Picayune* to the *New Yorker*, but at the end of his career he returned with a heightened sense of its meaning to the South of *The View from Pompey's Head* and *The Light Infantry Ball*. Such a list might be extended a great deal, but a sufficient number of writers have been named to indicate that the experience of the southern writer in going to the metropolis has a certain consistency.

It is not, therefore, surprising that Thomas Wolfe, one of the major southern writers, should have made the story of the Young Man from the Provinces in the great city one of the basic themes in his fiction. Indeed, after *Look Homeward, Angel*, which ends as Eugene Gant lifts his eyes upward and outward toward the North of which he has dreamed, Thomas Wolfe's work deals in large measure with the southerner in the city. First it is the city of Boston, then New York, then London, then Paris, and then Berlin, but always the intensely autobiographical record which Wolfe makes in his novels is a record of the outward movement of a southern boy from the mountains of North Carolina to the great cities of the world.

The story of this outward journey constitutes the greater portion of three massive novels which Thomas Wolfe produced after *Look Homeward, Angel*. In *Of Time and the River*, Eugene Gant leaves Altamont, travels to Boston, experiences "The coming on of the great earth, the new lands, the enchanted city, the approach, so smokey, blind and stifled, to the ancient web, the old grimed thrilling barricades of Boston . . . He saw the furious streets of life with their unending flood-tide of a million faces." In Boston, for the first time, he experienced the "fury" which the city created in him: "And from that moment on blind fury seized him. . . . Of this fury, which was to lash and drive him on for fifteen years, the thousandth part could not be told. . . . He was driven by hunger so literal, cruel and physical that it wanted to devour the earth and all things and people in it, and when it failed in this attempt his spirit would drown in an ocean of horror and desolation, smothered below the overwhelming tides of this great earth, sickened and made sterile, hopeless, dead with a stultifying weight of men and objects of the world, the everlasting flock and flooding of the crowd." Seldom has the intense involvement of a young provincial with a city been described in more extravagantly rhetorical terms than Wolfe uses here and throughout *Of Time and the River*.

In Boston Eugene Gant attends a great university, tries to understand the nature of life through watching his uncle Bascom Pentland, returns home to Altamont in the southern mountains on the occasion of the death of his father, and finds his sense of home sharpened and deepened by his experiences in the North. After completing his graduate work, he goes to New York City, teaches English in another university, and becomes acquainted with that most representative child of the city, Abe Jones. He also becomes acquainted with the rich and privileged people who live in the great houses along the Hudson River. Thus Boston and New York show him a rich culture and acquaint him with a great variety of urban people. In his friends Francis Starwick, in Boston (and later Paris), and Joel Pierce, in New York, he has guides who instruct him and open doors for him. Then he travels to Europe and has to find himself once more, this time in another, a different and, in many ways, richer culture than he had known before. First in London, then in Paris, and at last in southern France, as he came to know the land, the people, and their cultures, he came, too, to turn increasingly in upon himself. As he expresses it, "At morning in a foreign land, . . . he wakes and thinks of home . . . and the wilderness, the things that are in his blood, his heart, his brain, in every atom of his flesh and tissue, the things for which he draws his breath in labor, the things that madden him with an intolerable and nameless pain." In later works the extravagance of such rhetoric is to be reduced, but the essential situation there described does not change. No Young Man from the Provinces—in Stendhal, in Balzac, in Dickens, in Flaubert—has had his experiences of self-discovery and self-knowledge detailed more consistently, more thoroughly, or more passionately than Eugene Gant's are in *Of Time and the River*. The seeming lack of structure in the novel has puzzled its critics, leading them to seek new terms to use in characterizing it; Richard S. Kennedy, for example, has called it a *thesaurus* rather than a novel. However, when we look at the persistence in it of the theme of the Young Man from the Provinces, it becomes clearly a very loosely plotted example of that genre of fiction.

Wolfe was self-conscious about this pattern in his later fiction, as he was self-conscious about the Joycean pattern in *Look Homeward, Angel*. He says in *The Web and the Rock*, "There is no truer legend in the world than the one about the country boy, the provincial innocent, in his first contact with the city. . . . It has found inspired and glorious tongues in Tolstoy and in Goethe, in Balzac and Dickens, in Fielding and Mark Twain. . . . And day after day the great cities of the world are being fed, enriched, and replenished ceaselessly with the life-blood of the nation, with all the passion, aspiration, eagerness, faith, and high imagining that youth can know or that the tenement of life can hold." The further the Wolfe protagonists move into urban lives remote from the world of their childhood and youth, the more completely that world reasserts itself in memory in contrast to the city around them.

After *Of Time and the River* Wolfe abandoned Eugene Gant as his protagonist and substituted for him George Webber, who was the central figure in Wolfe's last two novels, *The Web and the Rock* and *You Can't Go Home Again*. *The Web and the Rock* in its early pages repeats in slightly modified form a brief record of the protagonist's childhood in what is now called Libya Hill, a mountain town in North Carolina, and his college experiences at Pulpit Hill. Then George Webber goes to New York City. Wolfe sees Webber's entry into New York in terms quite explicitly those of the story of the provincial in the city. He says, "For one like George Webber, born to the obscure village and brought up within the narrow geography of provincial ways, the city experience is such as no city man himself can ever know." And he adds, "When such a man, therefore, comes first

163

to the great city—but how can we speak of such a man coming first to the great city, when really the great city is within him, encysted in his heart, built up in all the flaming images of his brain: a symbol of his hope, the image of his high desire, the final crown, the citadel of all that he has ever dreamed of or longed for or imagined that life could bring to him? For such a man as this, there really is no coming to the city. He brings the city with him everywhere he goes, and when that final moment comes when he at last breathes in the city's air, feels his foot upon the city street . . . looks around him at the city's pinnacles, pinches himself to make sure he is really there—for such a man as this, and for such a moment, it will always be a question . . . which city is the real one, which city he has found and seen, which city for this man is really there."

This statement, with its clear juxtaposition of two cities—one of dreams and hopes, the other of actuality—defines one of the major themes of *The Web and the Rock* and its sequel *You Can't Go Home Again*, for they are accounts of George Webber's gradual and painful discovery that the two are not the same and that the first, tested by the second, always proves false. This steady testing process—which had been present for Eugene Gant to only a limited degree, chiefly in his sense of the suffering of the poor—seems always to turn the thoughts of George Webber back to the simplicity, beauty, and calm of the provincial world of his childhood. This theme, bluntly announced as George enters New York, is a dominant and shaping motif for the remainder of *The Web and the Rock* and for *You Can't Go Home Again*, where it is explained in great detail. In the latter novel George returns to the South briefly on the occasion of the death of his aunt, but the greater portion of the book deals with his experiences among the great and near-great in New York City, as the result of the success of his first novel and his entry into the world of artists, writers, and the theater through the tutelage of his mistress Esther Jack. Then he travels to Europe and in London meets Lloyd McHarg, plainly a fictional portrait of Sinclair Lewis. He travels on to Germany and in Berlin is forced into an acknowledgement of the darkness

and depravity which is, he now sees, a part of all human beings. Before the conclusion of this book he comes to recognize
that the city is not the enchanted place which he had once
dreamed that it was and which he had celebrated with much
passion on first approaching it. He sums up what the life of the
real city he now sees is through the representative figure of C.
Green, who commits suicide by leaping twelve stories from a
hotel to the street. He says of Green, "He was a dweller in mean
streets, was Green, a man-mote in the jungle of the city, a resident of grimy steel and stone, a mole who burrowed in rusty
brick, a stunned spectator of enormous salmon-colored towers,
hued palely with the morning. He was a renter of shabby
wooden houses. . . . He was a waker in bleak streets at morning." The world that C. Green commits suicide to escape is a far
cry indeed from the enfabled rock which Eugene Gant approached at the beginning of *Of Time and the River*, but in dis-
covering its nature, Wolfe's protagonists, and Wolfe himself,
were carried back closer to the simpler world of the South.

Provincials from other parts of the nation can approach New
York or Los Angeles much as provincials from Rouen approach
Paris or natives of Lichfield approach London, as in a sense
coming—"at last"—to their own capitals. Wolfe was intensely
aware of how different it was with southerners. He described
Webber's entry into the North, which for Wolfe was usually
synonymous with northern cities: "always the feeling was the
same—an exact, pointed, physical feeling marking the fron-
tiers of his consciousness with a geographical precision. . . . It
was a geographical division of the spirit that was sharply, physically exact, as if it had been severed by a sword. . . . He ducked
his head a little as if he was passing through a web." The metaphor of the web, in *The Web and the Rock*, consistently refers
to the South, as the metaphor of the rock refers to a metropolis.
The feeling Wolfe assigns his protagonist here is, he believes, in
no sense unique to Webber: "Every young man from the South
has felt this precise and formal geography of the spirit," he asserts, "but few city people are familiar with it." He speculates
on why this feeling is always there: ". . . they felt they were in-

vading a foreign country. . . . they were steeling themselves for conflict. . . . they were looking forward with an almost desperate apprehension to their encounter with the city." And he asks, "How many people in the city realize how much the life of the great city meant to him . . . how, long ago in little towns down South . . . something was always burning in [his] heart at night—the image of the shining city." Thus the southerner approaches the city as a foreign land and to some extent a hostile one. Perhaps because of the almost paranoid sense of being not merely provincial but an outsider, he remains, even over long periods of time, a sojourner.

Such a sojourner is different, and Wolfe explores the special characteristics that a southern provincial brings to this experience. George Webber decides that "there is no one on earth who is more patriotically devoted—verbally, at least—to the region from which he came than the American of the Southern portion of the United States. Once he leaves it to take up his living in other, less fair and fortunate, sections of the country, he is willing to fight for the honor of the Southland at the drop of a hat." He goes on to argue that a transplanted southerner is likely to be lonely in a great city and to look up others from his region and to "form a Community of the South which has no parallel in city life. . . . The most obvious reason for the existence of this Community is to be found in the deep-rooted and provincial insularity of Southern life." People from other regions are more readily and easily absorbed into the life of the city. The southerner, he says—and what southerner in a Northern city has not experienced it?—remains a stranger to some degree and always a sojourner. If Wolfe's account is that of the Young Man from the Provinces moving out to the great city, it is also an account of a man whose sense of the health, beauty, and dignity of the provinces grows steadily, first in contrast to the complexity and glitter of the great cities, then as a consolation to one lonely in the city as only in the city one can be alone.

Upon his death, Wolfe left the first ten chapters of an incomplete novel entitled *The Hills Beyond.* The story returns to the mountains of western North Carolina and to the kinds of people who had been a major part of the background of *Look Homeward, Angel. The Hills Beyond* is a story that celebrates the simple people of the mountain region. Gone now is much of the condescension and dislike which Wolfe had heaped upon them in *Look Homeward, Angel* and in the early pages of *The Web and the Rock.* Now he celebrates them as large folk characters drawn bigger than life with great gusto, vitality, and health. The author of this fragment had demonstrated very clearly that the further he got away from home and the more completely he realized the impossibility of attempting to go home again, the more vividly home and the South and its special qualities and characteristics existed in his mind.

The more deeply Wolfe became immersed in the life of the busy North, the more completely he became acquainted with and came to understand the rich culture of Europe, the more totally he described the interior life of his provincial protagonist as he confronted the great cultural centers of the world, the more a self-consciousness about his region grew in his own mind. Wolfe was very much the traditional southerner outside the South, one who is usually a recognizably uncomfortable creature whose southernness tends to become exaggerated. The comic figure of the "professional southerner" is a part of the response of this southern provincial to a world which is truly not his own, and the metropolis becomes for him a sounding board for realizing what his region truly is. Thomas Wolfe was thus both the major writer who most consistently used the frame of the southerner as provincial in the metropolis to order his work and the sharpest definer of the differences between that southern provincial and other American provincials approaching the great cities of the world. As the portrayer of that experience, he became the recorder of the common experience of many of his fellow southerners.

The Bildungsroman, *American Style*

In nineteenth and twentieth century German, British, and American writing, one of the most persistent forms has been the *Bildungsroman*, the novel whose prototype is generally considered to be Goethe's *Wilhelm Meister* and which deals with the growth to maturity of a young person, the development of his spirit, and the formation of a philosophy or world view which will enable him to function effectively as an adult.[1] The list of such works in English fiction is impressive both for their number and their quality, beginning with Book II of Thomas Carlyle's *Sartor Resartus*, which traces the spiritual development of Diogenes Teufelsdröckh, and continuing through Dickens's *David Copperfield* and *Great Expectations*, George Eliot's *The Mill on the Floss*, George Meredith's *The Ordeal of Richard Feverel*, Samuel Butler's *The Way of All Flesh*, Thomas Hardy's *Jude the Obscure*, James Joyce's *A Portrait of the Artist As a Young Man*, Somerset Maugham's *Of Human Bondage*, D.H. Lawrence's *Sons and Lovers*, and many, many more. These novels, however much they differ in many respects, all present the record of a young person who moves through a series of shaping or formative events to a position of philosophical stability and maturity.

In a sense, the *Bildungsroman* is usually a record of a series of rites of passage, of initiations for the young, unusually sensitive and intelligent protagonist, trials in which he is tested and instructed. Perhaps nowhere is this testing aspect of the *Bildungsroman* more obvious than in Joseph Conrad's short novel *The Shadow-Line*, in which the young hero in his first grim command makes the difficult movement from youth and illusion to maturity and knowledge. Frequently in these *Bildungsromane* there is a repetition of the pattern effectively described by Lionel Trilling as the story of the Young Man of the Provinces, the poor, naïve, but remarkably able and sensitive young protagonist who moves from provincial life to a major city and there encounters the tests which make or destroy him, protagonists such as Julien Sorel in Stendahl's *Le rouge et le noir* or Balzac's Eugène Rastignac in *Père Goriot* and several other novels in *La comédie humaine*.[2]

These *Bildungsromane* were by no means confined to Germany, France, and England. Indeed, the very nature of the American experience—that is, a new man in a new land, a man who can understand his own experience as well as his national and racial experience only by realizing himself through feats of strength or intelligence or endurance in rites of passage associated with wilderness, wild animals, wild men, and grim nature —seems to cry aloud for a literary form that emphasizes the road to self-discovery. And the American form of the *Bildungsroman* not infrequently is directly related to the British forms, as Thomas Wolfe's *Look Homeward, Angel* echoes James Joyce's *A Portrait of the Artist As a Young Man* structurally and thematically.[3] Nevertheless a significant number of American works have made modifications that are important and worthy of note in the structure and method of presenting the development of the sensitive young protagonist. Indeed, one may almost say that there is a special American form of the *Bildungsroman*.

In 1832, when Thomas Carlyle was seeking a publisher for his account of the spiritual growth of Teufelsdröckh,[4] Nathaniel Hawthorne in his short story "My Kinsman, Major Molineux" presented an account of an eighteen-year-old country boy, Robin Molineux, who goes to Boston sometime around 1740 to seek his fortune with the aid of his illustrious kinsman, Major Molineux. Robin is eager, enthusiastic, optimistic, poor, and ignorant—the provincial in every sense of the word—and he enters the city in perfect keeping with Lionel Trilling's picture of the Young Man from the Provinces. However, during his night in the city, nothing happens to him, except that he finds everywhere darkness, suspicion, hostility, and temptation. But he does not learn by succumbing to these things and experiencing them. He remains a wondering witness in a bewildering city, and at last he sees his kinsman, Major Molineux, tarred and feathered, being driven out of town by a jeering mob. Now disillusioned but wiser, Robin prepares to go back home. In that seemingly simple story, Hawthorne gave in almost schematic form a fundamental fictional statement about one important aspect of the American experience. A young, ignorant, idealistic, and optimistic provincial goes to the city, and there he has forced upon him a maturing awareness of the darkness and the evil potential in life; the story is very much like an episode in the tale of development which was popular throughout the western world.

What is remarkable about "My Kinsman, Major Molineux" is not this general theme, but the method by which Robin Molineux's rite of passage occurs. It comes not actually from his own experience or his own response to trials or actions or even from what is directly done to him, but from what he witnesses being done by and to others. The initiation through which he passes results from witnessing action not from taking it. That structure, in which a witness or a narrator watches actions by others and learns from them, has reappeared in so many American novels dealing with the maturing, development, or education of characters that it may be considered truly a peculiarly American form of the *Bildungsroman*.

I shall try to look briefly at a few representative novels by Americans which take this form with, of course, certain modifications. They are Herman Melville's *Moby-Dick* (1851), Nathaniel Hawthorne's *The Blithedale Romance* (1852), Henry James's *Madame de Mauves* (1873), *Daisy Miller* (1878), and *The Ambassadors* (1902), Willa Cather's *My Ántonia* (1918), and *A Lost Lady* (1923), F. Scott Fitzgerald's *The Great Gatsby* (1925), Allen Tate's *The Fathers* (1938), and Robert Penn Warren's *All the King's Men* (1946). In each of these works, the narrator or the viewpoint character witnesses the action of the protagonist in the main story, and from this observation gains an insight into the nature of experience. Ishmael, in *Moby-Dick*, for example, gains an attitude and a reconciliation to life through the actions which he witnesses Ahab performing. Coverdale, in *The Blithedale Romance*, comes to his adult position of tolerant cynicism about the possibilities of human reform through what he sees of the Blithedale experiment, and particularly Zenobia, Hollingsworth, and Priscilla, rather than through what he does in it. Longmore, in *Madame de Mauves*, learns from watching Eugénia de Mauves. Winterbourne is a witness to the tragedy in *Daisy Miller*. Lambert Strether comes to some self-knowledge and an aesthetic view of life in *The Ambassadors* through witnessing the affair between Chad Newsome and Madame de Vionnet. Jim Burden, in *My Ántonia*, comes to understand an element in life that has been beyond his personal experience through watching Ántonia, the Shimerdas, and the Bohemian girls. The meaning of *A Lost Lady* is registered through Niel Herbert. Nick Carraway, in *The Great Gatsby*, gains understanding through seeing the tragic disaster of Jay Gatsby. Lacy Buchan, in *The Fathers*, grows up through coming to understand, by observation, who and what George Posey is. Jack Burden, in *All the King's Men*, finds a philosophy of life from watching Willie Stark.

Melville and Hawthorne, in *Moby-Dick* and *The Blithedale Romance*, produced examples of the kind of novel of development about which I am talking, and between them they also showed the major variations in this form of the *Bildungsroman*. I shall, therefore, devote more attention to these two novels than to the other ones I discuss in this essay, because *Moby-Dick* and *The Blithedale Romance* are virtually archetypes of the form which I am attempting to define.

Moby-Dick embodies for this kind of *Bildungsroman*, as it does for many other aspects of the American novel, early examples of many of its characteristics. Because there are many aspects of the novel about which its numerous critics violently disagree, it may be well to set down a few commonly accepted facts about *Moby-Dick*. It is narrated by Ishmael, who is recounting events that happened "Some years ago, never mind how long precisely."[5] After an introductory fifth of the novel, once the *Pequod* "blindly plunged like fate into the lone Atlantic" (p. 197), the action of the story is centered, not on Ishmael and his philosophical quest (whatever it is), but on Captain Ahab and his mad pursuit of the great white whale, which is to him "the monomaniac incarnation of all those malicious agencies which some deep men feel eating in them. . . . That intangible malignity which has been from the beginning . . . all evil" (p. 160). This pursuit of Moby Dick leads to the destruction of the *Pequod* and all its crew except Ishmael.

Most critics and readers also agree that Ishmael's retrospective narrative of these events is told not only from the temporal vantage point of some years after they occur but also from the philosophical and spiritual vantage point which he has gained in part at least through the experience of the voyage. There is great disagreement about what that philosophical and spiritual position is. The interpretations cover a very wide range. Lawrance Thompson sees Ishmael's position as madness; William Ellery Sedgwick sees Ishmael as finally the center of a Dantesque *Divine Comedy*; I follow Howard P. Vincent and others in seeing Ishmael as reconciled to an incomprehensible universe of mixed good and evil; T. Walter Herbert, Jr., has recently argued lengthily the case of those who see Ishmael's final position as a skeptical nihilism, distrustful of all forms of truth.[6] There seems, however, little, if any, reluctance to see Ishmael as undergoing some significant and progressive change in philosophy or at least in attitude from the one he holds at the beginning of the novel.

At the opening, as I see the novel, Ishmael is properly named, for he is a spiritual outcast, alienated from his world, one who seems to feel that it may be said of him, as it was of his prototype, "His hand will be against every man"[7] and who sets sail on the *Pequod* as an act of symbolic self destruction: "With a philosophical flourish Cato throws himself upon his sword; I quietly take to the ship." (p. 12) Whatever we may believe the spiritual position of the mature Ishmael to be, the voyage has produced in him a great change; he has undergone great development;

and it is this mellowed and matured narrator whose voice tells the story and comments upon it and its meaning from time to time. These changes result not from Ishmael's actions or his decisions or his choices. He is the lowest ranking member of the crew of the *Pequod*, and he decides nothing about its course of action. The trial to which he is put is one which gives him little opportunity for choice or the exercise of his individual will. What he learns—and I believe he learns a great deal—he learns from watching Captain Ahab's actions, from vicarious but uncommitted participation in Ahab's mad quest. He escapes at last, I believe, because he has learned the lesson that "There is a wisdom that is woe; but there is a woe that is madness" (p. 355). He has learned the lesson of acceptance of the mixed good and evil in all things, of the prevalence of suffering in the world, of the horror in which at times the universe seems to be formed. These aspects of reality he has come to acknowledge without fright and without affront. What the *Pequod* and the mad quest of Ahab have taught him is the reality of evil in the world, the necessity of its being accepted and that a lowered "conceit of attainable felicity" (p. 349) is necessary if one is to live "in mute calm . . . while ponderous planets of unwaning woe revolve around him" (p. 326). Ishmael is very much like Diogenes Teufelsdröckh in these experiences, if I read the book right, for the voyage of the *Pequod* is truly a voyage through spiritual seas to a mature port for him.

What Ishmael witnesses on this voyage is evil as an active force, dark and destructive. The universe Ishmael sees is, indeed, "formed in fright," but Ishmael does not himself have to experience this universe personally, and he can, therefore, escape its direst consequences. In a sense, he does not himself undergo the rite of passage; he watches someone else undergo it and be destroyed by it.

There seems to be little question that Ahab is the protagonist of the novel, the "Catskill eagle" who is "higher than other birds upon the plain, even though they soar" (p. 355). Sedgwick properly calls him a Shakespearian tragic hero, but the method of telling the story, awkward as it sometimes becomes, invests the meaning and interpretation of this tragic hero in a very minor actor in the story, one who, through witnessing Ahab's tragedy, comes to terms with life. Those terms prove finally to be essentially domestic—"the wife, the heart, the bed, the table, the saddle, the fire-side, the country" (p. 349).

In one sense *Moby-Dick* can be summarized thus: a narrator tells the story retrospectively of how he watched a tragic figure pit himself destructively and madly against the evil of the world and how, through witnessing that action, he gained a philosophy of pragmatic acceptance, having come to recognize evil without himself having fully experienced its consequences. The concern of Ishmael in *Moby-Dick* is with the acceptance of an eternal cosmic aspect of man in an inimicable universe. The novel is laid in eternity, not time. When the *Pequod* plunges into the lone Atlantic, it moves back to primordial, primitive, pre-Christian existence. *Moby-Dick* asks Job's eternal question about the justice in human suffering, with its setting in something very like Job's patriarchal world of deserts and remote ages.

In *The Blithedale Romance*, on the other hand, the issue is firmly fixed in time and is defined, in part at least, by social history. Certainly the novel rests to an appreciable degree on Hawthorne's own experiences at Brook Farm. *The Love Letters* and *The American Notebooks* are proof enough of that.[8] But I believe that Leo B. Levy is correct in his insistence that the primary concern of the novel is not with the Brook Farm experiment so much as it is with "the central motivation of that enterprise—a desire to escape an encroaching technological and urban revolution and to preserve the agrarian ideal of an earlier America."[9] Its narrator, like Ishmael, I believe, learns a lesson of acceptance, but the lesson Miles Coverdale learns is to accept this inevitable technological revolution and to recognize what Levy calls the novel's theme "that the human heart cannot know itself well enough to enter the kingdom of heaven on earth."[10]

The narrator, in order to achieve emotional balance in his opposing desire for the older agrarian and pastoral way of life while he recognizes the new technological world he inhabits, escapes into an aestheticism. In every way what he sees and what he learns is a lesser, more restricted thing than Ishmael experiences. Coverdale is very much like one of Sir Walter Scott's heroes who occupy a historical neutral ground. Like them, he has a strong emotional attachment to the past and the pastoral, but, also like them, he is swept inevitably into the future, so that he seems, like Scott's weak protagonist, blown here and there by the winds of circumstance, faint in will and self-knowledge, gray in hue, and lacking luster.[11] Coverdale gives a retrospective narrative of the Blithedale experiment from the vantage point of ten years after the events, and his account reflects his skeptical and cynical acceptance of the impossibility of the experiment. He can wryly observe, "Whatever else I may repent of, therefore, let it be reckoned neither among my sins nor follies, that I once had faith and force enough to form generous hopes of the world's destiny."[12] He also declares, "I rejoiced that I could once think better of the world's improvability than it deserved" (p. 20). There has inevitably been great debate about the character of Miles Coverdale, about the accuracy of his judgments, and about the state of his mind at the time of the writing. Frederick Crews defined the basis of the problem well when he wrote: "Hawthorne is attempting what few writers have dared: a surface plot, an imaginative reconstruction of that plot by a narrator, and a symbolic commentary on both. . . . [the] narrator . . . is himself a subject of judgment."[13] This kind of narration and this sort of difficulty in interpretation we have seen before in *Moby-Dick*, where Melville presents us with Ahab's and Ishmael's views of the world and asks that we choose between them, and we shall see the same problem again in most of the novels discussed in this essay. Indeed, Crews's comment about the structure of *The Blithedale Romance* could be applied almost equally well to *The Great Gatsby*, *The Fathers*, or *All the King's Men*.

Such retrospective narration always creates epistemological problems. Irving Howe, for example, who believes *The Blithedale Romance* to be a failure, says "The trouble is not merely one of literary structure, it also involves a radical uncertainty as to the possibilities of knowledge."[14] But such difficulty is common in retrospective fiction where the attitudinal stance of the narrator is determined by what he has learned through the experience being recounted. The demands of storytelling require that he tell the events in seriatim order with their outcome withheld, but his evaluation of these events is reflected in style, metaphor, and statement. When this principle is violated, as Ishmael violates it at the end of the first chapter of *Moby-Dick*, the reader's credence in the novel is not enhanced but weakened. To be puzzled, therefore, about a retrospective narrator's telling the story as though he did not know what happened next, is to fail to appreciate the basic demands which narrative suspense make upon a narrator.[15]

The basic points about *The Blithedale Romance* as an example of a witness's *Bildungsroman* are: The fundamental plot is the tragic triangle of Zenobia, Hollingsworth, and Priscilla, with Westervelt operating as a kind of almost mechanical devil or figure of evil. That plot ends in disaster, death, and self-recriminations and demonstrates the grim presence of evil even in a newly made Eden. Coverdale is an observer who feels for and learns from these people but is not a part of their experience. He says at one point, "My own part, in these transactions, was singularly subordinate. It resembled that of the Chorus in a classic play, which seems to be set aloof from the possibility of personal concernment, and bestows the whole measure of its hope or fear, its exhaltation or sorrow, on the fortunes of others, between whom and itself this sympathy is the only bond. Destiny . . . seldom chooses to arrange its scenes, and carry forward its drama, without securing the presence of at least one calm observer. It is his office to give applause, when due, and sometimes an inevitable tear, to detect the final fitness of incident to character, and to distil in his long-brooding thought, the whole morality of the performance" (p. 97). It is from his position arrived at from having distilled "in his long-brooding thought the whole morality of the performance" that Coverdale is telling this story, and whatever we may think of the spiritual position he occupies at the end of the Blithedale experiment, it is certainly different from that which he had had at its beginning, and that difference is a function of what he witnessed at Blithedale. Thus in a radically different kind of novel from *Moby-Dick*, one with a much more circumscribed theme and field of action and one whose protagonist is in maturity a minor poet and a confirmed cynic, Hawthorne has used the same essential shape that Melville did.

Richard Poirier, who sees *The Blithedale Romance* in a somewhat similar way, concludes that Coverdale has created, by a form of aestheticism, "an environment for the self rather than submitting to the environment authorized"[16]; thus Coverdale becomes a prophetic "example of the particular kind of sensibility that was to find fuller expression in those crucial years 1890–1914."[17] To Poirier "Coverdale is an anticipation of the hero of *The Ambassadors*."[18] But James had in fact been using Coverdale-like observers for a long time before he reached his "major phase," and sometimes these observers were cast in roles that correspond closely to what I am calling the witness character in the American-style *Bildungsroman*. Such characters control the narration in two of his early nouvelles, *Madame de Mauves*, written in 1873, and *Daisy Miller*, published serially in 1878, the work which was to prove James's first real popular success.

In each of these short novels the viewpoint character, an American living in Europe, meets an American woman who personifies the innocence and the freedom of the American people, watches a series of events in which this American woman is the central figure and to which the witness has only incidental and peripheral relationships, falls in love, in some fashion, with the American woman, and sees the basic situation in which the woman is involved end tragically, in both cases with someone's death. Out of witnessing these experiences the observers come to understand themselves and the meaning of American innocence and moral passion much more clearly than they had at the beginning. Everything we learn about the central plots we learn through their mediation, observation, or interpretation, but both Longmore, in *Madame de Mauves*, and Frederick Winterbourne, in *Daisy Miller*, are passive characters to whom nothing really happens in the action of the story. Longmore is persuaded to propose an affair to Eugénia de Mauves with the approval of her wayward husband, but she firmly rejects him. Winterbourne does not recognize until the die is cast and the opportunity is no more that he is in love with and attracted by the innocence and the freedom of Daisy Miller, but when he learns it, it is too late. Madame de Mauves's firm American morality forces her to refuse to forgive her husband when he repents of his affairs, and thereby she drives him to suicide. This adamant stand leads Longmore to look with something like a fearful awe upon the effects of the morality that Madame de Mauves imposes upon her world. Daisy Miller, defying the conventions of expatriate American society, goes walking in the Coliseum at night with an Italian gigolo and there catches her death of Roman fever. Winterbourne, a thoroughly expatriated American, as a result of her death finds himself unhappy with the nature of the life of his fellow expatriates and concludes, "I have lived too long in foreign parts." Rather than going back to America, as Longmore had done in *Madame de Mauves*, however, he returns to Geneva.

An argument might be made that neither Longmore nor Winterbourne in these two *nouvelles* really learns a great deal by experience or that what they learn is in fact connected only with manners, with patterns of social conduct. To argue this, however, is to open once more the argument of whether James is able truly to invest mores and social conventions with deep thematic and philosophical significance. I believe that he is. If we assume that both Longmore and Winterbourne are different, wiser, and more mature people after they have watched Eugénia de Mauves and Daisy Miller in these two stories, then we must see these stories as being to some degree short novels of development in which a spectator character learns primarily by watching. In each case the spectator character is weak in will, passive, incapable of firm action, and in a kind of ambiguous love relationship to the heroine of the story, and in each case the darkness which is lurking beneath the surface of even the most firmly fixed social conventions has erupted, destroying others rather than the witness but instructing that witness in a dark dimension of life which that witness might otherwise never have seen. A different kind of character, indeed one somewhat like Madame de Mauves or Daisy Miller, appears as the observer in *The Ambassadors*, but the role he plays is startlingly similar.

On the surface *The Ambassadors* seems to be a strange novel to group with *Bildungsromane* concerned, as the form usually is, with the experiences of adolescence and young manhood. Lambert Strether is a middle-aged widower, the editor of a small, very intellectual review, and a person sent as his fiancée Mrs. Newsome's ambassador to save her son Chad from the perils of an illicit love affair in Paris. However, Strether, despite his age, approaches Paris very much like the innocent young provincial approaching the city. His innocence is essentially the American innocence, resting upon high idealism and the lack of a fully developed aesthetic sensibility. In this sense he approaches Paris as innocently as Robin Molineux had approached Boston. Furthermore, Strether fits the pattern of the protagonist of a *Bildungsroman* because of his sensitivity, his imagination, his capacity for precise observation, and his tendency toward moral inquiry. That his intellectual and aesthetic maturity comes to him late in his physical life is the basis for the tragic part, if indeed such there be, of this ironic comedy. *The Ambassadors* is a tale of lost innocence and of confusions about the nature both of the innocence and the loss. Chad Newsome's innocence has already been lost quite literally, with results that at least initially seem to Lambert Strether to be good. Strether's intellectual and moral innocence in turn is lost, and he must reconcile his strong Puritan moral sense with his growing knowledge of that lost innocence.

What ultimately is instructed, however, is not Lambert Strether's moral sense but his aesthetic sense, so that, like Miles Coverdale, though with radically different results, Strether's story is the story of the education of a sensibility. Hence, *The Ambassadors* has at least some of the characteristics of the *Künstlerroman*, the story of the development of an artist. The story is told so completely from Strether's point of view that there is great disagreement among critics and readers about the meaning and the theme of *The Ambassadors*, about what Paris means, about whether or not Strether's story is a story of renunciation, or of moral growth, or is a satire on the Puritan way of life, or a description of the corruption inherent in Paris, or a variety of other things. The world is seen as he sees it and the movement of the plot so clearly reveals that Lambert Strether has a genius for misinterpretation that the reader is left to make his own conclusions about the book, and most of them can be supported by some evidence within the text, ranging from F.R. Leavis's conclusion that Paris is taken "too much at the glamorous face value"[19] to Joan Bennett's claim that "the Paris he renounces for himself contains cruelty, grief, and suffering as well as generosity, courage, and joy."[20] But however much critics may differ about the meaning of Paris and of Strether's experience, there is a pretty common agreement that the book is an account of the education of its protagonist, an idea expressed very emphatically by Walter F. Wright among many others, when he said "*The Ambassadors* might have been called 'The Education of Lambert Strether,' for the other ambassadors from America to Europe served merely to contrast with Strether and we are interested in his ambassadorial mission only because it is basic to his acquisition of knowledge."[21] F.O. Matthiessen wrote of "Strether's gradual initiation into a world of new values."[22] Christof Wegelin refers to "the crisis in Strether's education."[23] And almost everyone sees the book in terms somewhat like these.

But the education which Strether gains is not an education through acts he performs himself but an education of his sensibility and imagination through what he sees in Paris and what he sees of the affair between Chad Newsome and Madame de Vionnet. About this, too, there is virtually complete agreement among the critics. Leon Edel says "It is *seeing* that is the subject of the novel."[24] Joan Bennett says that we share a "whole series of impressions with the protagonist."[25] Wegelin says, "At the end Strether *sees*, and we are interested in *what* he sees. 'The business of my tale and the march of my action, not to say the precious moral of everything,' James says again, 'is just my demonstration of this process of vision,' and his emphasis falls both on *process* and on *vision*."[26]

It is Madame de Vionnet who is the most instructive of all things seen for Strether, for the central problem that he confronts in the book is that of understanding who and what she is and somehow coming to terms with her life and her beauty. As Wegelin has well noted, what shocks Strether is "seeing into the very depths of common human weakness" and thereby learning that "the woman whose beauty is the main cause of his new vision is after all not proof against defeat and pain."[27] Richard Poirier has seen the entire novel as being "essentially about . . . the process of 'conversion': the failed 'conversion' of Chad by Madame de Vionnet, the 'conversion' of Strether by Paris into a man whose capacities for appreciation create a world —alternative both to Paris and to Woollett . . ."[28] and he finally sees Strether's generosity being "betrayed by the materials—like Chad—on which it has expended itself."[29]

In a sense *The Ambassadors* has the structure of a detective story—indeed there is an element of the detective story structure in all these special kinds of *Bildungsromane*; for the detective story consists of a major plot laid in the past that culminates in a crime and then the uncovering and understanding of the nature and meaning of that plot through a second plot laid in the present by someone not himself directly involved in it, usually the detective, who must piece together the materials of the past events into some meaningful and intelligible pattern. For Lambert Strether, who does not at first recognize that a mystery exists, the change in Chad Newsome and the attractiveness and charm of Madame de Vionnet present a mystery. That mystery he gradually tries to unravel. At last all the facts about that mystery are in his hands, and he must place upon them a meaning. That meaning seems to be that there must be in life somehow a meaningful merging of aesthetic and moral principles. As is typical of most detective stories, this kind of plot owes a great deal to James's absorption of his brother William's philosophy of pragmatism. Indeed, in one sense *The Ambassadors* may be regarded as a novel which rests upon the process of perception, and it could be considered a very long fable illustrative of William James's "The Will to Believe." For example, the recognition scene of the novel, which occurs in chapters 3 and 4 of Book Eleventh, is a scene in which Strether sees the physical clues which lead him to understand that the nature of the liaison between Chad and Madame de Vionnet was guilty. The recognition scene does not bring Strether to a knowledge of himself or his own actions but to an understanding of the relationship of the people whom he has been watching, and, significantly for the aesthetic nature of this work, it is a scene which Strether views not directly through his own perceptions but through an aesthetic frame. He sees it, indeed, as being like a small painting by Lambinet which he had seen in Boston years before and had, he thought, forgotten. Thus in his own mind he sees Chad and Madame de Vionnet alone in the canoe on the lake in what is a compromising relationship through the frame of aesthetic appreciation and at the same time the memories of the Boston from which he came. Having witnessed this scene, Strether must now go through one of James's typical interior actions, in which he must somehow take his old beliefs that had been firmly held and gradually modify them in the light of the new facts forced upon him until he can reach a new conclusion that is in some way emotionally commensurate with both the things that he wills to believe and the facts that have been forced upon his attention. The entire book functions this way, and Lambert Strether, who finishes the story educated to an imaginative response and an artistic sensibility radically different from any that he could have known in Woollett or Boston, has gained these new attitudes by being a passive observer rather than an active agent. Hence, however much his story differs from that of Ishmael or Miles Coverdale, the three of them share a common relation to the experiences which most emphatically modify their attitudes toward the experience of living. That relationship is one of passive observation rather than active participation.

In *The Ambassadors*, a story told in the third person through the sensibilities and observations of a middle-aged observer, it is necessary to justify declaring it to be, as I believe it is, an example of what I am calling the American-style *Bildungsroman*. Not so with Willa Cather. Two of her very best books so clearly fit the shape and structure which I have been attempting to describe that one may almost feel that she is consciously working in the tradition. These are *My Ántonia*, published in 1918, and the superb short novel *A Lost Lady*, which was published five years later.

My Ántonia is an account of the childhood, adolescence, and young adulthood of Ántonia Shimerda Cuzak, as viewed from the vantage point of twenty years after by Jim Burden, who grew up with her. Jim is the grandson of a well-established Nebraska family, and he has all the advantages which wealth and position can offer one on the Nebraska plains. Ántonia is the daughter of a poor Bohemian immigrant family. At the time of the narration of the story Jim's life has moved from countryside to the small town of Black Hawk, from there to the University of Nebraska, from there to Harvard, and now he is living in New York City as the attorney for one of the great western railroads. In all this movement from the early history of the nation, represented through the first farming settlements, back eastward through the stages of history to the nation on the verge of the First World War, Jim has had success, but his marriage is without children and unhappy; his life is somehow empty; and when he looks back upon the path which he has followed, he is haunted by the attraction of an earlier, simpler life closely associated with the soil, a life represented by Ántonia. The novel is his account of what *his* Ántonia has meant to him. Although Willa Cather in an interview said that Jim "was to remain a detached observer, appreciative but inactive, rather than take a part in [Ántonia's] life,"[30] the novel is, as many critics have pointed out, a double story in which Jim Burden is far too important to be merely the narrator of someone else's life.[31] The more closely we look at the novel, the more important and central Jim's role appears, for Ántonia tends to become, as David Daiches has noted, "an objectification of the observer's emotions . . . her growth, development, and final adjustment is a vast symbolic progress interesting less for what it is [sic] than for what it can be made to mean. . . . Throughout the book the narrator's sensibility takes control."[32] Jim is much more than a narrative device; he becomes a fundamental element in the theme, which is essentially that described in the epigram on the title page, "*Optima dies . . . prima fugit*," the best day flies first. He is the medium for expressing this recognition of the nostalgic sense that, as the obligations of civilization and history increasingly impress their weight upon the individual, they carry him further and further away from the good, simple, and pastoral life of which Ántonia remains a hardy representation.

Perhaps the most famous metaphor in the novel is the one which occurs at the end of chapter 14 of Book II, in which Jim and the hired girls, on a picnic see a plough that "magnified across the distance by the horizontal light [of the setting sun behind] . . . stood out against the sun, was exactly contained within the circle of the disk; the handles, the tongue, the share —black against the molten red. There it was, heroic in size, a picture writing on the sun."[33] This symbolic representation of the heroic days of the West before the coming of everything that Jim's later life is to represent, most of the critics have praised for its beauty and its promise of optimistic strength. They have failed to read the paragraph which follows it: "Even when we whispered about it, our vision disappeared; the ball dropped and dropped until the red tip went beneath the earth. The fields below us were dark, the sky was growing pale, and that forgotten plough had sunk back to its own littleness somewhere on the prairie."[34] This awareness of darkness approaching, of the diminished possibilities of the simple and primitive, of the cost which the severe struggle will exact is firmly impressed upon Jim Burden, primarily through his long and affectionate regard for the hard life of Ántonia. At the end of Book I, when Ántonia is talking with Jim at his grandfather's home, she says, "'If I live here, like you, that is different. Things will be easy for you. But they will be hard for us.'"[35] And indeed so they proved to be.

John H. Randall III is only partially right when he says, "The use of a double protagonist has certain advantages: it allows one character to be an actor and the other a spectator; one can be youth which performs and accomplishes unthinkingly, the other middle age which can interpret the significance of action in others but itself has lost the capacity to act."[36] More is at stake in *My Ántonia* than the contrast between the active and the contemplative life. Ántonia represents the strength, the freedom, and the fecundity—in the final book she is virtually an Earth Mother—which opened the frontier and built the West, and with courage and enormous vitality survived scorching summers and the grimness of winter. Jim represents that diminished quality which follows upon the early triumph of vigor and action. The emotion which this book consistently evokes is that of nostalgic longing, of the backward look toward the lovely and lost past. At the conclusion Jim, a somewhat cynical and successful man, looks back to say, "I had the sense of coming home to myself, and of having found out what a little circle man's experience is."[37] This attitude is quite comparable to that of Miles Coverdale, though Coverdale came to distrust the pastoral element in life and Burden has to come to distrust the to-him-necessary urban element. But the emotion which floods the book is not this distrust but a sense of the beauty of what is lost: "Whatever we had missed, we possessed together the precious, the incommunicable past."[38]

In 1923 in her nearly perfect short novel *A Lost Lady*, Willa Cather repeated this theme of the decline of the western virtues and the western order. She repeated, too, the pattern of the boy and young man who learn about themselves and the nature of life from witnessing the career of someone else, in this case that of Marian Forrester, a kind of midwestern Madame Bovary. *A Lost Lady* differs from *My Ántonia* structurally in many ways but not in the role of the witness, despite the fact that the book is told in the third person rather than the first. Niel Herbert, the witness, comes finally to understand that he has been a part of a heroic age and that through witnessing the decline and moral fall of Marian Forrester he has seen a symbol of its sad decline. He concludes near the end of the novel, "This was the very end of the road-making West. . . . It was already gone, that age; nothing could ever bring it back. The taste and smell and song of it, the visions these men had seen in the air and followed,—these he had caught in a kind of after glow in their own faces,—and this would always be his."[39]

The lesson that Jim Burden and Niel Herbert both learn in these novels of the decline of the Golden Age of the West is, like Ishmael's and Coverdale's, a lesson of acceptance, but what is accepted is not a cosmic order of the universe nearly so much as it is a view of history. In a small sense both of these novels have protagonists who come to have as knowledge brought painfully to the heart a sense of history that was common at the time of the writing, a sense that owes much to Henry Adams and Spengler.[40]

When F. Scott Fitzgerald was struggling with the structure and organization of *The Great Gatsby*, he found illumination in method and structure through looking at other writers. He himself acknowledged debts to Joseph Conrad's Preface to *The Nigger of the Narcissus*.[41] Other obvious sources aided him in arriving at the structure of his novel, including Conrad's stories in which Marlow serves as narrator, notably *Lord Jim* and *Heart of Darkness*; but he found in Willa Cather's *My Ántonia* and *A Lost Lady*, as James E. Miller points out, sources which were structurally very helpful to him.[42] The problem he confronted was how to tell the story of James Gatz, his powerful love for Daisy Buchanan, and the force with which he struggles against all limitations to realize his own impossible dream of success in life and love, and at the same time to make him a symbol of America in the 1920s and, by some extension, a symbol of American history. In other words, how to invest Gatsby's story with the meaning which Fitzgerald wants the reader to carry away. In order to accomplish this, Fitzgerald used double protagonists, with Nick Carraway serving as the narrator who attempts to solve the mystery of who and what Jay Gatsby is.

Carraway is another of the provincials entering the city, a midwestern boy who comes to New York and is awed by his relatives Tom and Daisy Buchanan and by the nature of life on Long Island and in Manhattan. Through the experiences that he witnesses but participates in only peripherally, Nick is led to a sense of the moral decay that is in this eastern world, and at the conclusion, he "wanted the world to be in uniform and at a sort of moral attention forever."[43] He extended this view of the world he sees and this sense of Gatsby's impossible dream to a statement about American history and one that differs relatively little from the one that Willa Cather made in *My Ántonia* and *A Lost Lady*: "I became aware of the old island here that flowered once for Dutch sailors' eyes—a fresh, green breast of the new world. Its vanished trees, the trees that had made way for Gatsby's house, had once pandered in whispers to the last and greatest of all human dreams; for a transitory enchanted moment man must have held his breath in the presence of this continent, compelled into an aesthetic contemplation he neither understood nor desired, face to face for the last time in history with something commensurate to his capacity for wonder."[44] This metaphor, even more famous than Miss Cather's plough against the sun, says essentially the same thing about the decline of the West, but Nick Carraway differs from Jim Burden and Niel Herbert in one important respect: having come to the city and seen "what foul dust floated" there, he has rejected the city and has returned to the Middle West, having learned, he feels, much about "the abortive sorrows and short-winded elations of men."[45]

Much has been written in an effort to understand which is the dominant story in *The Great Gatsby*, Gatsby's or Carraway's, and what the book means, but in at least one sense *My Ántonia*, *A Lost Lady*, and *The Great Gatsby* are stories that have a common concern with the shape of history and present that concern through witness characters who are peripheral to

187

a pattern of action that describes the essential darkness and decay settling upon the land.

That concern with the shape of history is even greater in Allen Tate's *The Fathers*, a novel which might be taken as a paradigm of the American-style *Bildungsroman*, if for no other reason than the explicitness of its own comments about its form. The novel is laid in Virginia and Washington just before and during the Civil War. Its protagonist is George Posey, an outsider, a man of action, a "new man," who does not understand the complex society of Virginia. The narrator defines "what the Poseys had lost;" it was, he said, "an idea, a cause, an action in which his personality could be extinguished."[46] The central action poses this man deeply committed to his private, individual emotions and values against the old order of Virginia society, in which the individual found his value in his relation to the social order: "Our domestic manners and satisfactions were as impersonal as the United States Navy, and the belief widely held today, that men may live apart from the political order, that indeed the only humane and honorable satisfactions must be gained in spite of the public order, would have astonished most of the men of that time . . ." (pp. 125–26). The events which occur are catastrophic, and they create an atmosphere of evil. The narrator says: "To hear the night [which, he feels, modern men cannot do] . . . one must have deep inside one's secret being . . . a belief in the innate evil of man's nature, and the need to face that evil, of which the symbol is darkness, of which again the living image is man alone" (p. 219). By "man alone" he means George Posey, of whom he says, "[George] is alone. He is alone like a tornado. His one purpose is to whirl and he brushes aside the obstacles in his way"(p. 268).

The narrator of this story is Lacy Buchan, a retired physician who is telling these events as he remembers them from a time fifty years before, when he was fifteen and sixteen. He defines himself as "an unmarried old man . . . [who] has a story to tell. Is it not something to tell, when a score of people whom I knew and loved, people beyond whose lives I could imagine no other life, either out of violence in themselves or the times, or out of some misery or shame, scattered into the new life of the modern age where they cannot even find themselves?" (p. 5). Referring to boys of his age at the outbreak of the Civil War, he says, "We had our own excitements . . . but this is not my story" (p. 152). In terms that almost constitute a definition of the American-style *Bildungsroman*, he says, "I mark the beginning of my maturity with a scene, and another marks its completion, and you will understand that neither of them properly speaking was an experience of my own, but rather something sheer, out of the world, easier to bring back than the miseries and ecstasies of my own life" (pp. 117–18). Lacy is equally clear about what he learned from what he witnessed: "There was of course no one moment that it was all leading up to, and that piece of knowledge about life, learned that day, has permitted me to survive the disasters that overwhelmed other and better men, and to tell their story. Not even death was an instant; it too became a part of the ceaseless flow, instructing me to beware of fixing any hope, or some terrible lack of it, upon birth or death, or upon love or the giving in marriage" (p. 101).

This process of interpreting actions and declaring their meanings is, of course, made possible by the double perspective of Lacy Buchan, who at one point in the novel, says, "In my feelings of that time there is a new element—my feelings about that time: there is not an old man living who can recover the emotions of the past; he can only bring back the objects around which, secretly, the emotions have ordered themselves in memory" (p. 22). The story he tells is what he witnessed stated as a function of the meaning it had in the process of his maturing. As such *The Fathers* is a highly personal *Bildungsroman*. The story it tells of the Buchans and the Poseys—the events which Lacy witnessed—is a commentary on history and a condemnation of the present through a portrayal of a past that is better. As such it shares with *My Ántonia, A Lost Lady,* and *The Great Gatsby* a pastoral nostalgia for a lost better world.

Robert Penn Warren's concern with the meaning of history is well known, and he has explored it in a variety of forms and modes. What is almost universally recognized as his finest work, *All the King's Men*, explores this concern through the commenting, speculative narration of a minor actor in the drama. In one sense, much of Warren's work has been concerned with the initiation of a protagonist, certainly in *Night Rider, At Heaven's Gate, World Enough and Time, Wilderness,* and *A Place To Come To*; but the one being initiated is a central actor in all these novels, with the partial exception of *At Heaven's Gate*, where Bogan Murdock is a far more important character in the main plot than Gerald Calhoun, who is undergoing the rite of passage.

In *All the King's Men* the dominant character is Willie Stark, and the principal action is his rise to political power, his career as governor, and his tragedy. Stark is like Captain Ahab or Jay Gatsby or Marian Forrester or George Posey—a powerful central figure who absorbs the interest and attention of the narrator and the reader. But the novel is told in the first-person as a retrospective narration by Jack Burden, for whom the events of Stark's political career become the means of Burden's coming to a reconciliation with a very imperfect world of very imperfect men. *All the King's Men* is a long and very complex novel, and Jack Burden has a more significant role to play in its plot than most of the witnesses at whom we have been looking, although his role is still minor in the central plot. What gives him his centrality to the novel is his style—brash, metaphysical, and nervous—and the skeptical philosophical attitude which he takes toward both himself and events. In these respects he is much like the narrator of Teufelsdröckh's life in *Sartor Resartus* or like Ishmael.

Warren uses a special device to establish Burden's mature stance. Years before the time of action of the Willie Stark plot, when Burden was a graduate student in history, he had done research for his dissertation on Cass Mastern, a man who had died in the Civil War. But a kind of intellectual ennui had set in and he abandoned the project. He could read the words, he tells us, but "how could he be expected to understand them? They could only be words to him, for to him the world then was an accumulation of items, odds and ends of things like the broken and misused and dust-shrouded things gathered in a garret. Or it was a flux of things before his eyes (or behind his eyes) and one thing had nothing to do, in the end, with anything else."[47] The Cass Mastern material is a grim story of a man who hated slavery and freed his slaves, fell in love with another man's wife, committed a murder, and finally died in the Civil War, in his death expiating his sin. It finally comes to have for Burden, working expediently and cynically in Stark's political machine, a powerful meaning. When he reviews Cass Mastern's life in the light of his own experiences, he says, "Cass Mastern lived for a few years and in that time he learned that the world is all of one piece. He learned that the world is like an enormous spider web and if you touch it, however lightly, at any point, the vibration ripples to the remotest perimeter and the drowsy spider feels the tingle and is drowsy no more but springs out to fling the gossamer coils about you who have touched the web and then inject the black, numbing poison under your hide. It does not matter whether or not you meant to brush the web of things. Your happy foot or your wing may have brushed it ever so lightly, but what happens always happens and there is the spider, bearded black and with his great faceted eyes glittering like mirrors in the sun, or like God's eye, and the fangs dripping" (p. 200). He is now aware of the imperfection of all things and of the inevitable complicity of man in all events. He has learned this lesson from Willie Stark, Judge Irwin, and Adam and Anne Stanton, and he can apply it not only to his old dissertation subject but also to himself and his world. In this hard-won maturity he can declare, "If you could not accept the past and its burden there was no future, for without one there cannot be the other, and . . . if you could accept the past you might hope for the future, for only out of the past can you make the future" (p. 461). He is now ready, he declares, to "go into the convulsion of the world, out of history into history and the awful responsibility of Time" (p. 464). The course he has followed is a familiar one; we have seen in it most of the novels discussed in this essay. The world he has witnessed, like the worlds of our other observers, has forced him to see the dark and tragic underside of life. And the conclusion he has reached in his maturity is to accept the terms of existence. Jack Burden, like the others, has had the good fortune to go to school and learn by example rather than experience directly the tragic potential of life.

If I am correct in believing that this special form of the novel of development has appeared in American writing often enough to constitute a subgenre of the *Bildungsroman*, the question of why raises itself. Any answers are, of course, speculative, but two suggest themselves.

One, I believe, has to do with the desire which Hawthorne expressed in *Mosses from an Old Manse* "to achieve a novel that should evolve some deep lesson and should possess physical substance enough to stand alone."[48] Or as Allen Tate said of his intention while writing *The Fathers*, "I tried to make the whole structure symbolic in terms of realistic detail, so that you could subtract the symbolism, or remain unaware of it, without losing the literal level of meaning . . . but if you subtract the literal or realistic detail, the symbolic structure disappears."[49] For Hawthorne in *The Scarlet Letter* the use of what F.O. Matthiessen called "the device of multiple choice,"[50] together with the declared ignorance of the narrator, forces the reader into seeing "some deep lesson." In *The Blithedale Romance* the retrospective narrator can assign meanings and interpretations without violating dramatic propriety, as can—and does—Ishmael, in *Moby-Dick*, Jim Burden, in *My Ántonia*, Nick Carraway, in *The Great Gatsby*, Lacy Buchan, in *The Fathers*, and Jack Burden in *All the Kings Men*. All are first-person retrospective narrators, who not only establish an angle of vision for the reader but are expected by the reader to speak from a position of understanding achieved through the events being described. In the other novels discussed the witness characters are presented as centers of consciousness through third-person narration. The reader sees the action as that character sees it and is informed of that character's interpretation of it and, to some extent at least, its effect upon him. The roles of Longmore in *Madame de Mauves*, Winterbourne, in *Daisy Miller*, and Strether, in *The Ambassadors*, are not unlike Niel Herbert's role in *A Lost Lady*; all struggle to understand a baffling lady and are informed and matured by what they understand. Willa Cather says of Niel, "He came to be very glad that he had known her, and that she had had a hand in breaking him in to life."[51]

Viewed in this sense, then, the use of the witness character is a technical strategy on the part of the novelist, an attempt to allow the reader to remain within the created universe of the fiction and still to be instructed in how to understand it. The use of this witness character enables the novelist to control the "deep lesson" of his work without having, in Arthur Mizener's words, "To sacrifice a probable presentation of the shows of things to the direct expression of what the novelist thinks the things mean."[52]

Such an explanation accounts, at least to some extent, for the use of the retrospective witness character, but it does not account for the frequency with which American characters in the *Bildungsroman* reach their mature attitudes as a result of what they see rather than what happens to them or what they do.

One possible explanation is that this form reflects the unconscious conflict in a group of American writers between the essentially optimistic demands of the novel of development and a sense of the tragic quality of life. If the protagonist is to learn a mature response to life, he must face the darkness, pain, and injustice that are large elements of living, and he must survive it with the possibility of actually achieving his lowered "conceit of attainable felicity." In novels laid in the complex social structures of Europe and England, this learning process could and often did take place without violence. In the simpler, cruder, and more violent world of America, such darkness and evil were likely to find their expression through extreme violence and death or physically and spiritually destructive actions. The frequency of death or extreme violence in these novels is very high; only in *The Ambassadors*—in many respects a social novel —is it not a significant part of the central action. In each of these *Bildungsromane* the witness character is forced to see, through what happens to others, the "power of blackness" in his world. And in all these cases he takes an essentially American attitude toward it, an attitude of pragmatic acceptance. Having seen examples of the mines in the field of life, he does not—like most of the protagonists in the central plots of these novels—push on with blind or ideal courage. Instead, he tries to come to terms with this newly recognized reality and, in typical American fashion, to find a way to "make do."

Notes

1. I am relying primarily on three sources for information about the *Bildungsroman*. In order of their importance to me, they are Susanne Howe, *Wilhelm Meister and his English Kinsmen: Apprentices to Life* (New York, 1930); G.B. Tennyson, "The *Bildungsroman* in Nineteenth Century English Literature," *Medieval Epic to the "Epic Theater" of Brecht: Essays in Comparative Literature*, ed. Rosario P. Armato and John M. Spalek (Los Angeles, 1968), pp. 135–46; and Jerome H. Buckley, *Season of Youth: The Bildungsroman from Dickens to Golding* (Cambridge, Mass., 1974). Tennyson has a fine summary of German criticism and definitions of the term. I have not followed his effort to discriminate among *Bildungsroman*, *Entwicklungsroman*, *Erziehungsroman*, and *Künstlerroman*, but have assumed, as he seems to, that *Bildungsroman* is the generic term and the one commonly used in English criticism to include all the others. My loose definition has debts to all three sources, although I am sympathetic with—and indeed use, as Tennyson does—the idea that some kind of spiritual or philosophical development is usually characteristic of the form.

2. Lionel Trilling, *The Liberal Imagination: Essays on Literature and Society* (Garden City, N.Y., 1953), pp. 67–73.

3. Richard S. Kennedy, "Wolfe's *Look Homeward, Angel* as a Novel of Development," *South Atlantic Quarterly* 63 (Spring, 1964), 218–26.

4. Tennyson sees *Sartor Resartus*, Book II, as the English beginnings of the *Bildungsroman*, except that it asserts philosophical change rather than presenting such change novelistically (pp. 140–41).

5. Herman Melville, *Moby-Dick: An Authoritative Text*, ed. by Harrison Hayford and Hershel Parker (New York, 1967), p. 12. All quotations are from this edition and pages will be given parenthetically in the text.

6. Lawrance Thompson, *Melville's Quarrel with God* (Princeton, 1952); William Ellery Sedgwick, *Herman Melville: The Tragedy of Mind* (Cambridge, Mass., 1944); C. Hugh Holman, "The Reconciliation of Ishmael: *Moby-Dick* and the Book of Job," *South Atlantic Quarterly* 57 (1958), 477–90; Howard P. Vincent, *The Trying-Out of Moby Dick* (Boston, 1949); T. Walter Herbert, Jr., *Moby-Dick and Calvinism* (New Brunswick, N.J., 1977).

7. Genesis 16:12.

8. See particularly, Nathaniel Hawthorne, *The American Notebooks*, ed. Claude M. Simpson (Ohio State Univ. Press, 1972), 196–222. Hubert H. Hoeltje, *Inward Sky: The Mind and Heart of Nathaniel Hawthorne* (Durham, N.C., 1962), pp. 382–95, examines in detail Hawthorne's use of personal experience in the novel.

9. Leo B. Levy, *"The Blithedale Romance"* Hawthorne's 'Voyage Through Chaos,'" *Studies in Romanticism* 8 (Autumn, 1968), 4.

10. Ibid.

11. Alexander Welsh, *The Hero of the Waverley Novels* (New Haven, Conn., 1963); C. Hugh Holman, "*Nigel* and the Historical Imagination," *The Classic British Novel*, ed. H.M. Harper and Charles Edge (Athens, Ga., 1972), pp. 65–84.

12. Nathaniel Hawthorne, *The Blithedale Romance* and *Fanshawe* (Ohio State Univ. Press, 1964), p. 11. All quotations are from this Centenary Edition; pages will be given parenthetically in the text.

13. Fredrick C. Crews, "A New Reading of *The Blithedale Romance*," *American Literature* 29 (May, 1957), 1969.

14. Irving Howe, *Politics and the Novel* (Greenwich, Conn., 1967), p. 170.

15. William C. Spengemann, in *The Adventurous Muse: The Poetics of American Fiction, 1789–1900* (New Haven, Conn., 1977), disastrously constructs a large and untenable thesis about American fiction on his failure to recognize this principle. See particularly pp. 186–88, where he builds an intricate theory on Tommo's apparently not knowing how the *Typee* experience will work out.

16. Richard Poirier, *A World Elsewhere: The Place of Style in American Literature* (New York, 1966), p. 123.

17. Ibid., 115.

18. Ibid.

19. F.R. Leavis, *The Great Tradition* (New York, 1963), p. 161.

20. Joan Bennett, "The Art of Henry James," *Chicago Review* 9 (Winter, 1956), 26.

21. Walter F. Wright, *The Madness of Art: A Study of Henry James* (Lincoln, Nebr., 1962), p. 232.

22. F.O. Matthiessen, *Henry James: The Major Phase* (New York, 1944), p. 19.

23. Christof Wegelin, *The Image of Europe in Henry James* (Dallas, Tex., 1958), p. 93.

24. Leon Edel, "Introduction," *The Ambassadors* (Riverside Ed., Boston, 1960), pp. xv.

25. Bennett, p. 26.

26. Wegelin, p. 89.

27. Ibid., p. 104.

28. Poirier, pp. 130–31.

29. Ibid., p. 136.

30. E.K. Brown, *Willa Cather: A Critical Biography*, completed by Leon Edel (New York, 1958), p. 202.

31. Among the many who have pointed out this structure, perhaps the most important—and detailed—statement is by John H. Randall III in *The Landscape and the Looking Glass: Willa Cather's Search for Value* (Boston, 1960), pp. 107ff.

32. David Daiches, *Willa Cather: A Critical Introduction* (Ithaca, N.Y., 1951), pp. 44, 45.

33. Willa Cather, *My Ántonia*, Sentry Ed. (Boston, 1961), p. 245.

34. Ibid.

35. Ibid., p. 140.

36. Randall, p. 107.

37. Cather, pp. 371–72.

38. Ibid., p. 372.

39. Willa Cather, *A Lost Lady* (New York, 1973), p. 172.

40. Both Adams, in *The Degradation of the Democratic Dogma* (1919), and Spengler, in *The Decline of the West* (1918), saw civilization as a running down of a vast machine because of the use of its irreplaceable energy. Adams applied the second law of thermodynamics to history as an explanation of this decline.

41. In the Introduction to the 1934 Modern Library Edition of *The Great Gatsby*.

42. James E. Miller, *The Fictional Technique of F. Scott Fitzgerald* (The Hague, 1957), pp. 79–81; Andrew Turnbull, *Scott Fitzgerald* (New York, 1962), pp. 150–51, 342; Kenneth Eble, *F. Scott Fitzgerald* (New York, 1963), p. 87.

43. F. Scott Fitzgerald, *The Great Gatsby*, Scribner Library Ed. (New York, 1953), p. 2.

44. Ibid., p. 182.

45. Ibid., p. 2.

46. Allen Tate, *The Fathers* (Denver, Colo., 1960), p. 179. All quotations are from this edition and page references will be given parenthetically in the text.

47. Robert Penn Warren, *All the King's Men* (New York, 1946),

p. 201. All quotations are from this edition and page references will be given parenthetically in the text.

48. Nathaniel Hawthorne, "The Old Manse," *Mosses from an Old Manse* (Boston, 1883), p. 13.

49. Quoted in Arthur Mizener, *The Sense of Life in the Modern Novel* (Boston, 1964), p. 170.

50. F.O. Matthiessen, *American Renaissance: Art and Expression in the Age of Emerson and Whitman* (New York, 1941), pp. 276–77.

51. Cather, *A Lost Lady*, p. 174.

52. Mizener, pp. 268–69.

Index

This index contains the names of persons and titles appearing in the text. It does not list subjects or footnote references. Works are listed under their authors' names.

198

Windows on the World

Longstreet, Augustus Baldwin 29, 32, 33, 35, 36
  WORKS: *Georgia Scenes* 29, 33, 35
Lorre, Peter 73
Lubbock, Percy 20
  WORKS: *Craft of Fiction, The* 20
Lukács, Georg 122, 123
  WORKS: *Historical Novel, The* 122

Macaulay, Thomas Babington 13
McCall's 75
Mark Twain 15, 49, 86, 163
  WORKS: "Man That Corrupted Hadleyburg, The" 49
Marquand, Adelaide Hooker 72–73, 80
Marquand, Christina Sedgwick 68, 72
Marquand, John Phillips 15, 23, 61–97
  WORKS: *B. F.'s Daughter* 76, 77, 87, 91, 93
  Black Cargo, The 70, 77
  Castle Sinister 74
  "Deep Water" 72
  Don't Ask Questions 74
  Four of a Kind 69, 70
  "Fourth Down" 72
  "Golden Lads" 72
  "Good Morning, Major" 72
  Haven's End 70, 71, 83, 91
  "High Tide" 72
  H. M. Pulham, Esquire 75, 76, 86, 92–93
  It's Loaded, Mr. Bauer 76
  "King of the Sea" 79
  Last Laugh, Mr. Moto 73, 76
  Late George Apley, The 61, 62–63, 64, 71, 72, 74, 75, 77, 82, 83–85, 87
  Late George Apley, The (play, co-author) 76, 82
  Life at Happy Knoll 61, 80
  Lord Timothy Dexter of Newbury-port, Mass. 70
  Melville Goodwin, USA 78–79, 87–88

Marquand, John Phillips (*cont.*)
  Ming Yellow 72
  Mr. Moto Is So Sorry 73, 74
  No Hero 73
  Only a Few of Us Left 70
  Point of No Return 71, 77–78, 87, 89, 94
  "Rainbows" 72
  Repent in Haste 76
  Sincerely, Willis Wayde 80, 82, 88, 91, 94
  So Little Time 70, 76, 77, 87, 89, 93–94
  Stopover: Tokyo 74, 80, 95–96
  "Sun, Sea, and Sand" 79
  Thank You, Mr. Moto 73, 74
  Think Fast, Mr. Moto 73, 74
  Thirty Years 72, 79
  3-3-8 74
  Timothy Dexter Revisited 70, 81, 83
  Unspeakable Gentleman, The 67, 77, 83
  Warning Hill 70–71, 77, 91
  Wickford Point 61, 62, 74, 75, 85–86, 93
  Women and Thomas Harrow 61, 80, 88, 91–92, 94, 96
Marquand, Philip 64
Marx, Karl 123
Masters, Edgar Lee 50–51
  WORKS: *Spoon River Anthology, The* 50–51
Matthiessen, F. O. 180, 192
Maugham, W. Somerset 85, 168
  WORKS: *Cakes and Ale* 85
  Of Human Bondage 168
Melville, Herman 11, 95, 99, 138, 170, 171–174, 175
  WORKS: *Moby-Dick* 5, 11, 18, 19, 138, 170, 171–174, 175, 176, 177, 192
Meredith, George 102, 103, 168
  WORKS: *Ordeal of Richard Feverel, The* 168
Miller, James E., Jr. 186
Millgate, Michael 134
Milton, John 119
  WORKS: *Paradise Lost* 119

202

Windows on the World

Windows on the World has been composed on the Compu-graphic phototypesetter in 10-point Caledonia with two-point spacing between the lines. Palatino Italic was selected for display. The book was designed by Cindy Rampey, typeset by Metricomp, Inc., printed offset by Thomson-Shore, Inc., and bound by John H. Dekker & Sons.

The University of Tennessee Press : Knoxville

"Every novel is a window on the world," observes C. Hugh Holman. In this collection of essays—four of which are published here for the first time—the distinguished literary critic turns his attention to windows on a social world, in the American realistic novel from the last quarter of the nineteenth century to the present.

Against the currently fashionable argument that the traditional form of the American novel is the romance, Holman's opening essays argue for the significance of realism as a fundamental American literary mode. He then treats American humor and the novel of manners, examining such writers as Erskine Caldwell, Flannery O'Connor, Ring Lardner, Sinclair Lewis, and Ellen Glasgow. Four essays are devoted to particular variations in the realistic mode; such as Glasgow's use of history, Faulkner's expressionistic distortion of reality, the extent to which Wolfe (a deeply romantic writer) was dominated by his editor, and the way in which he explored the European realistic genre that dealt with the provincial in the city.

The volume concludes with an attempt to isolate a particularly American narra-